Years Ahead

Years Ahead

ROBERT DOUGALL
and the Years Ahead team

Editor Rosemary Forgan

Ward Lock Limited · London
in association with
Channel Four Television Company Limited

Acknowledgments

The publishers would like to thank the following for
supplying photographs for the book.
Horticultural Therapy 62, 63 below; Saga 32; Shirley
Seaton 27, 31; Sidhartha Films 7, 16, 23, 25, 34, 35,
38, 58, 63 top, 68, 69, 72 top and below, 78, 79, 82, 86,
87; *Yours* newspaper 9, 18, 19, 24, 26, 85, 90.

Cover photograph by Tom Mannion
Line drawings by Kevin Maddison

The *Years Ahead* team:
Rosemary Forgan
Ian Hazleton
Rosemary Hargreaves
Simon Passmore
Shirley Seaton
Anne Whitehouse

Years Ahead is made by Sidhartha Films in association
with Channel Four Television Company Limited.
Producer Steve Clark-Hall

© Sidhartha Films Limited and Robert Dougall 1984

First published in Great Britain in 1984
by Ward Lock Limited, 82 Gower Street,
London WC1E 6EQ, a Pentos Company.

Text set, printed and bound by
Netherwood Dalton & Co. Ltd. Huddersfield

British Library Cataloguing in Publication Data

Dougall, Robert
  Years ahead.
    1. Retirement—Great Britain
    2. Aged—Great Britain—Life skills guides
    I. Title
646.7'9'0941   HQ1064G7

ISBN 0-7063-6300-0

Contents

Introduction
Robert Dougall

'That's the way it is tonight, from the Newsroom and from me – Goodnight.'

Sounds more like an ending than a beginning, doesn't it? Yet for me, New Year's Eve, 1973, was the beginning of one of the busiest and most interesting periods of my life – retirement.

Some people shudder at the very word, while others look forward to it eagerly as the start of a wonderful long holiday. I certainly hope we can convince you, in the following pages, that there is less reason to shudder than you supposed, and as for holidays – have you ever had that terrible experience when you wake up on the first morning, in a beautiful location, dazzling sunshine, you amble slowly down to breakfast and strike up a conversation with some pleasant people on the next table. Then, horror of horrors, you find they are staying in the same hotel, they flew in on the same plane, but their holiday cost them £50 less?

Well, retirement can be a bit like that. It is certainly an excursion into foreign territory, and there are so many things to do and so much enjoyment to be had, but if you do not know where to look (or what you are entitled to), you can end up missing out. You need to plan it more carefully than any holiday, and in this book we hope to give you a few pointers; some ideas you may not have thought of, a few areas of help you may not know about.

In my own case, I had been working for the Beeb for forty years. I still felt fighting fit and full of go – but where? After all that time, building up a relationship with millions of viewers, suddenly to stop – the idea was very strange and would have been traumatic for me, had I had nothing to fill that void. But more of that later.

You may decide to sit and read this book from cover to cover, or you may want to dip into it from time to time as new situations arise.

Far be it from me to give any detailed advice. The distinguished contributors will be doing that in the pages that follow. Viewers of the Channel 4 programme, *Years Ahead*, which I present each Tuesday, will already feel they know many of them from their regular appearances.

All I want to say now is – plan it right and retirement can be a wonderfully rewarding time. Make the most of every one of those years ahead.

1   Preparing for Retirement

Kay Sykes

Many people behave as if retirement were some unpleasant disease, not to be spoken of until too late for treatment. How wrong they are! Retirement is a natural progression from one chapter of life to another, and should be accepted as such. But obviously, as with all other major changes – moving to a new school, choosing a job or career, marriage or starting a family – the better planned it is, the more enjoyment we will derive from it.

And those who go on planning and adapting *throughout* their retirement are those who enjoy it most of all.

So what do we mean by retirement planning? Spring cleaning, perhaps! In the old days, this meant a complete upheaval in the home. Everything was turned out, room by room, given a thorough clean and put back with some adjustments. A good housewife had the whole operation planned like an army manoeuvre. And that is what we are talking about now, because in many respects, retirement is very similar.

WHERE TO BEGIN?

With ourselves. Probably the most difficult thing to assess is how we appear to other people. How would our partners describe us? We might get a nasty shock! To get the best out of retirement, flexibility is essential. Have we become very set in our ways over the years? If so, we must rectify this and make room for new ideas, accepting the fact that patterns change and we must change with them. In the past, we were motivated by our full-time employment, but now we must pause and think about the future. And for once a degree of introspection is needed: What do I really enjoy doing? Are there unfulfilled hopes and ambitions I might tackle now?

It makes me angry when people say, 'What can

Kay Sykes.

you expect at our age', when they have been disappointed over some experience. What we can expect depends entirely on our own attitude, and the initiative and effort we put into living.

Retirement has changed completely in concept within the last decade; it comes earlier to many and can easily bring disillusionment. It may be closely related to redundancy or unemployment, and has to be approached in the same way. Are we going to join those who think it is not worth trying any more? Or do we say, 'Retirement is going to work for us and we are going to enjoy it'? The latter, I hope.

Some months ago, I received a letter from one of our viewers of *Years Ahead*, who started thus: 'I am a senior citizen of some experience', and continued: 'The great psychological trauma on retirement is status loss, and it needs tolerance and a strong character, with some humour to overcome it.' A wise man! Having worked for the same firm, or in the same job, for some years, it is very daunting to leave its protection and face the outside world. Everyone knew us within our department or circle of workmates, and none of that will count any more. We are facing a new chapter: to some enormously exciting, and to others a cause of panic.

One dictionary definition of 'panic' is: 'a sudden fright, particularly without real cause; terror inspired by a trifling cause'. It should have no place in the mind of the retirement planner. So many people make wrong decisions through fear – fear of poverty, fear of isolation or negative living. If we proceed carefully over our planning, taking each worry out into the open and studying it with quiet common sense, we should find the pattern to suit our personal circumstances.

No one is alone in retirement; it affects husbands and wives, sons and daughters and sometimes our parents as well. So discussion about future plans is essential. Too often throughout life, husband and wife get along quite comfortably without discussing anything very much; each partner taking it for granted that the other knows what is wanted, without being told. Now is the time to make extra sure that everyone is in on the act. It is wrong to think that other people do not want to share in our worries, and it is not fair to leave them in the dark regarding our apprehensions. So let us get down to some straight talking; we shall come up with some satisfactory and, sometimes, surprising answers.

Sharing the responsibility of running the home comes first, and this *can* be tricky. To husbands and wives, I would say: do not try to change things overnight, whether it is budgeting, administration or physical labour. However, this can be an ideal time for each partner to let the other one in on some aspects of 'their job'. To husbands: you may well be around for another forty years to mend the fuses, but it will not do any harm if your wife knows how to do it too. And to wives I would say: if your husband shows some interest in cooking, do not, for goodness sake, turn his offer down. It may take a while for him to catch up with your high standards – after all, you have had a head start – but it can be very reassuring to know that if you have to rush off and visit a sick friend, in another part of the country, he can cope (well, just about!) on his own.

What do you want from the future? Peace and quiet or stimulation, study and travel? Are you going to need some discipline in your life, some specific job, working in a particular routine again? When there is too much time it is easy to say, 'I'll do it tomorrow'. And that particular tomorrow never comes! We also need to justify our existence and retain relationships with the people around us. However comfortable your own home, life is nothing if you cut yourself off from the community – remember, we are talking about retirement from a particular job, not from life itself. Whatever you are looking for, you will probably find some ideas you had not even considered in the chapter entitled 'A Reason to Get Up in the Morning'.

Whatever you plan to do, you cannot get very far without money, and loss of earnings is a cause of real concern for many. Again, sit down with the family and work out what is coming in, from pensions, savings and so on, and what is going out on living expenses. There is a guide to help you on pages 40-1. And you may well find that you are better off than you expected. How many people look at their pay packets in detail? For my part I was only interested in the final figure in the bottom right-hand corner! But what about all those sums that were taken off: national insurance, pension payments, union dues, club subscriptions and so forth, to say nothing of income tax. The 'take-home' pay is all we are really interested in and many, even high-earners, have been pleasantly surprised by the final analysis. Chapter 3 looks at all aspects of money.

Obviously our homes and gardens need attention, and it may be that some of us have ambitious plans for these, which will keep us occupied for a long time. Nevertheless, let us also look outwards

Sid Rooksey waged a one-man campaign, which included writing to the council and to his MP, to have the local beach made safe for children to play on. When he resorted to clearing up the rubbish himself, he attracted plenty of helpers.

and see what is going on around us. Wherever we live, there is enormous scope for voluntary work (dealt with more fully on page 16), but think also about local commitments, such as activities within the Church, parish council or community centre, sports clubs and other clubs for the young, the old and the handicapped, to say nothing of conservation and neighbourhood enterprises. Again, my advice would be to proceed with care and not to become too involved too quickly. The danger is that to take on too much is almost as bad as doing nothing at all, as it completely destroys the enjoyment of leisure. To join local clubs is not expensive and is one of the best ways of making new contacts and spreading one's wings. In larger towns there are theatre groups, music societies, art centres, museums and the like, all crying out for friends and members. Time after time in the following pages we mention the Citizens' Advice Bureaux; there is bound

to be one near you and, together with the local library, they are a mine of information about all that is going on locally.

Retirement is a great leveller, and role reversal one of the most interesting aspects of it – the businessman into bricklayer, and labourer into Open University graduate. Many find fulfilment in their hidden attributes, using skills that they were hardly conscious of. But there are very few people who know exactly what they want to do immediately on retirement. That is why it is essential to take time to look around, and not rush into the first thing available. Some are very fortunate in having built-in hobbies and interests, but there are many who have given their whole being to their full-time career – particularly those who live alone – and for whom starting anew is difficult.

Perhaps the most pressing question for many is where to live. To move or stay put? This is dealt with in detail in Chapter 4. Even if you are one of those people who simply loves moving, make sure you think carefully – not just about the sort of home you want now, but about one that will suit your needs in ten or fifteen years time. Again, the very best advice is to talk it through with your nearest and dearest, taking into account their needs and desires for the future as well as your own. It can be a great adventure for a couple to move, if it has been properly talked through and thought about – and the financial aspect taken into account. If you have been in the same house for many years, you may have forgotten just how expensive moving can be. It is not only the actual money involved in selling one house and buying another through solicitors' and estate agents' fees. What of the cost of moving furniture and effects, the expense of, possibly, keeping two homes going for a while; to say nothing of maintaining dependants, and even boarding fees for a cat or dog.

More and more people decide against a move. If that is so in your case, now is the time, preferably before retirement, to look at your home objectively and see what can be done to improve it to suit future requirements. Details of the areas you may wish to consider (and ways of raising the money) are given later in the book, on pages 50-4. In addition to major improvements, this is also a good time to look around within the home: could you do with a new cooker; are the carpets becoming threadbare and therefore potentially dangerous? Much better to get these things put right in advance of retirement if at all possible, while you are still earning. A friend of mine started a second bottom drawer a year before her husband retired, and month by month renewed old and worn household linen (our towels have certainly seen better days!), replaced kitchen utensils and brought her pots and pans up to date.

Health is obviously of prime importance in retirement, and this is dealt with in Chapter 5. So often the media tends to concentrate on two distinct extremes when it comes to retired people: either as old and decrepit in geriatric wards, or that small minority who are still climbing mountains at ninety-three. In between are millions of people enjoying good health and active lives far into old age. Remember that only 2 per cent of the millions of retired people in Britain actually do finish their days in a geriatric ward, and although we cannot all hope to scale mountains (whatever our age), there is no reason to let our health become an all-consuming worry. Chapter 5 also looks at ways of staying fit, and what action you can take if you feel you are not getting a fair deal from the NHS.

Retirement is a misleading name for a time of life which can be just as active as that which has gone before. It is impossible to lay down rules for a happy retirement as so much depends on individual needs and aspirations, but from my own experience in helping people who are coming up to retirement, or indeed are well into it, the happy ones are those who use their leisure to the full. 'All work and no play makes Jack a dull boy' – and that goes for the pensioner also. How many of us have said in our lives, 'I would do that – if only I had more time'. Now we can prove that we meant it, and that we did not use our full-time work as an excuse not to play an active part in life around us.

2   A Reason to Get Up in the Morning

Robert Dougall

One of the things you may be looking forward to in retirement is the simple matter of not having to set the wretched alarm clock at the crack of dawn to get you up for work. Yet, paradoxically, the one thing that *everyone* needs when they retire is some reason to get up in the morning.

Whether you decide to go on working, or to fulfill an old ambition to find out more about your ancestors, or whether it is simply the scraping of paws against the front door reminding you that dogs have no concept of 'retirement' whatsoever – the fact is you will certainly feel much better if there is something standing between you and the temptation to lie in bed until lunchtime.

As I mentioned earlier, I became extremely busy in those first months of 1973, working on my autobiography, which I had started some time before. I called it simply *In and Out of the Box*, and to my total amazement, it went into ten editions and then into paperback.

Perhaps my own eagerness to get started on something completely new stemmed from an incident more than twenty years earlier. My wife, Nan, was a young war widow when I married her in 1947, and I found myself with not only a wife, but also a ready-made daughter aged three. We lived at that time in a ground-floor flat in London's West Hampstead. As the nearest open space happened to be a cemetery, and as we had a small puppy called Larry, we used to walk there quite often. One day, as we passed two crumpled old people sitting on a stone bench among the gravestones, little Miche looked at me and piped up at the top of her voice: 'Daddy, is that where people sit when they are waiting to die?' I bustled her away, hoping the old folk had not heard. All the same, I remember the occasion as though it were yesterday, and I vowed there and then to live each day to the full.

In the pages that follow, there is a wealth of suggestions for things to do. In fact, if you were to take up only a few of the suggestions you might end up wondering how on earth you ever found time to go out to work.

Another job: paid or voluntary?

Kay Sykes

The dictionary defines work as the 'effort put out to make or achieve something', and that 'something' is all important. Everybody's circumstances in retirement are different, but certain ground rules apply to all. For this reason you need to do some homework before you present yourself in the market place.

WHY DO WE WANT A JOB AT ALL?

There are three principal reasons for continuing to work:

Money

This is probably the first reason that springs to mind. Retirement comes so much earlier to many people now, and there may still be dependant children, mortgage commitments and other payments to worry about. At the same time, everyone wants to avoid having to drop their standard of living.

It may sound a silly question, but have you considered whether you really *need* extra money? Or is it that your self-esteem is linked to the amount of money someone is prepared to pay you? If you are *not* determined to find paid employment, the choice of employment opportunities available to you is far wider and may provide greater scope for enjoyment.

If you decide you definitely want paid work, part-time or full-time, you must consider another factor: the *earnings rule*.

This will affect you if you are a man aged sixty-five to seventy, or a woman aged sixty to sixty-five. Under this rule, you can earn up to a certain amount each week (currently £65), and still draw your basic state pension in full. But once you earn more than that amount, a proportion of your state pension is *lost*. A job that pays £65 a week, plus travelling expenses and a subsidized canteen, would make you better off than one which paid several pounds more. (Full details of the earnings rule, and 'cancelling' your retirement, are given on pages 42 and 39.)

Stimulation and involvement

In addition to money, a job can provide other important benefits: a feeling of involvement, a sense of achievement when things go well, mental stimulation, and the companionship of the people we work with.

At some point in their lives most people half consider the idea of a totally different job: one they feel they would derive more satisfaction from. Often it is dismissed because 'It wouldn't be so well paid' or 'It doesn't have much security'. If you are receiving sufficient pension to cover your living costs, *now* is the time to explore these avenues.

Time

Thirdly, on retirement, everybody will find they have extra time on their hands. Even if you have an all-consuming hobby or interest, maybe the idea of the discipline, the basic routine, of a job – perhaps for just one or two days a week – still appeals.

WHAT SORT OF JOB TO LOOK FOR?

Once you have given some consideration to *why* you want a job, the next question is: what sort of job, and how to go about finding it? There are three categories of work available: full-time or part-time salaried jobs; voluntary work; self-employment.

It is crucial at this stage to discuss all plans with the family and decide which pattern of work fits in with all requirements.

Also, do ask for advice – people love giving it,

and you do not have to take it. But someone may suggest an idea that had not occurred to you.

Finally, do read *all* the sections on employment opportunities – even if you have already made up your mind about what you want. The line dividing paid work from the voluntary sector is becoming increasingly smudged these days. For instance, British Executive Service Overseas (BESO) is really a voluntary organization, yet they will organize air fares (for you and your partner), living accommodation and expenses of £25 a week, if you use your management, professional or technical skills on one of their 'assignments'. These assignments consist of a three-month or four-month stay in a developing country, where experienced professionals are desperately needed to advise and set up local businesses. (More details on page 15.)

Paid work: full-time/part-time

Kay Sykes

Make it known to all friends and relations, colleagues at work and every contact you can think of, that you are in the market and seriously looking for something to do. Put out feelers as soon as possible; preferably while still in employment as prospective employers then know that skills are up to date, and that you still have the discipline of a working day. You would have to be living on another planet not to know that the employment market is tight now; and to be honest, full-time jobs – that suit you exactly – can be hard to find at any age. To your advantage, chances are you have plenty of contacts, and as we all know, jobs often go to a 'friend of a friend'. Do what you can to make sure *you* are that friend.

JOB CENTRES

Some are good, some appalling, depending upon who is running any particular one and where it is, but it is always worth going to see what is on offer. Never say about anything, 'Oh, it's not worthwhile going to see them – they won't want me at my age'; there is always the chance that you will be in the right place at the right time, and from my own experience in the recruitment field I know that older candidates have quite often been successful over younger ones, particularly in part-time jobs with small firms. Job Centres have undergone considerable changes recently, partly because of the recession. Many small firms now give their vacancies to them instead of to private agencies because of expense, and there are many more opportunities for part-time, short-term contract and temporary work than there were. Without doubt, those are the areas in which retired people are going to be most successful. Do not turn up your nose at temporary work; it can often lead to a permanent appointment, possibly in a more responsible position. I know one woman who got her temporary post twenty years ago – and she is still there. 'Temps' are never asked their age, and once established in a firm nobody even notices.

The address of your local Job Centre will be in the telephone book.

PROFESSIONAL AND EXECUTIVE RECRUITMENT SERVICE (PER)

This is a Government-run organization offering employment in the professional, executive, scientific and technical fields. They publish *Executive Post* weekly, and it is sent free of charge to all who register, either through one of their thirty-five centres or through the local Job Centre. The service is really for those who 'retire' early, as you cannot use the service if you are already receiving a state pension.

PER
Head Office,
Moorfoot,   phone: Sheffield
Sheffield S1 4PQ.   (0742) 753275

SUCCESS AFTER SIXTY

Despite its name, this organization will consider people under sixty. It specializes in office work: anything from tea ladies to accountants.

Success After Sixty,
40/41 Old Bond Street,
London W1X 3AF.   phone: 01-629-0672

33 George Street,
Croydon,
Surrey.   phone: 01-680-0858

EXECUTIVE STAND-BY

This is a specialized agency finding short-term contracts for 'mature people of 45+'. It has particular contacts within the petro-chemical industry, and also offers some overseas postings.

Executive Stand-by
310 Chester Road,
Hartford,
Northwich,
Cheshire CW8 2AB.   phone: (0606) 883849

Executive Stand-by (South) Ltd
91 London Wool and Fruit Exchange,
Brushfield Street,
London E1.   phone: 01-247-5693

Executive Stand-by (West) Ltd
Somercourt,
Holmfield Road,
Saltford,
Bristol.   phone: (02217) 3118

THE JOB-CHANGE PROJECT

Birmingham Settlement,
318 Summer Lane,
Newtown,
Birmingham B19 6RL.   phone: Birmingham
(021) 359-3562

EMPLOYMENT FELLOWSHIP

This organization runs small workshops for retired and disabled people throughout Britain. Although the rates of pay are not high, they aim to develop a pleasant and 'club-like' atmosphere.

An offshoot of the Employment Fellowship is Buretire, an expanding employment agency which aims to match up retired people from all walks of life with prospective employers for part-time work. Not only do the centres find jobs for retired people, but they are also looking for managers to run new centres.

Employment Fellowship,
Drayton House,
Gordon Street,
London WC1H 0BE.   phone: 01-387-1828

Buretire: same as Employment Fellowship.

AGE CONCERN

Some Age Concern branches run employment bureaux as well as all their other functions. The number of your local branch will be in the telephone book.

EXACT

This stands for Executives In Action, which they obviously are because new branches are springing up all the time. They not only offer jobs to members, but also advise on becoming self-employed or starting up a small business. EXACT was set up by two Rotary Club members in Yorkshire, three years ago. To find out if there is a branch in your area (or maybe you would like to start one), contact your local Rotary Club (the number will be in the telephone book).

For ex-servicemen and women there are two organizations which offer full- or part-time work.

Royal British Legion Attendants Co. Ltd,
2 Southend Crescent,
London SE9.   phone: 01-859-5621

Corps of Commissionaires,
3 Crane Court,
Fleet Street,
London EC4.   phone: 01-353-1125

The latter will also accept retired civil servants, police officers, coastguards, firemen and so on.

ACTION IN RETIREMENT

This is a relatively new organization setting up local groups which work on the premise that there must be thousands of retired plumbers and builders without work, and thousands of retired people wanting to avoid the infamous 'cowboy' builders. There is no faulting the principle, but reports coming in to *Years Ahead* are very mixed as yet. While the members seem to be getting a good service there are, to say the least, teething problems with the franchise operators. (See also the section on Franchises, page 17).

In addition to the above suggestions, it obviously makes sense to look in your local paper, and at notice-boards in the post office or newsagents. Do study the small print and beware of those that say 'suitable for retired person'. As like as not, this means that they are not prepared to pay the proper rate for the job.

On the whole, it is not advisable to place advertisements offering your services in a newspaper, unless it is a professional or trade paper where you are more likely to attract the attention of people interested in your particular background.

Voluntary work

Kay Sykes

If you are still labouring under the delusion that voluntary work always means taking round cups of tea in hospital or organizing soup-kitchens, make sure you are sitting down when you read this because you are in for quite a shock.

One of the few spin-offs of recent government cut-backs has been the vast mushrooming of ideas and schemes in the voluntary sector. Of these one of the most imaginative is:

REACH

This stands for Retired Executives Action Clearing House. Based in a rather grim building in Holborn, it acts as a nerve-centre for the rest of the country matching up retired people who have a mass of different skills to offer with a number of interesting organizations that simply cannot afford 'paid help'.

Although the work is not paid as such, most of the projects will reimburse travelling expenses and some offer other facilities, such as a subsidized canteen or luncheon vouchers. However, it is the sheer scope of the jobs on offer that makes REACH so exciting.

The wonderful thing about REACH is that the people running it really do practise what they preach. The office is totally run by 'retired' people: their press officer is a former provincial newspaper editor, and one of their computer 'match-makers' freely admits that the only thing he knew about typing – until he went to REACH – was that the typing pool was where the prettiest girls were to be found.

Lots of little boys dream about running their own railway. Then, when they grow-up they choose something more 'sensible'. Like Richard Wright who became a cost surveyor and materials controller with a construction company. But now at sixty-four Richard does have his own railway to run: the Leighton Buzzard Narrow Gauge Railway, which carries 10,000 paying passengers each year. Richard started off by helping with administration and looking after stock in the small gift shop. Because you cannot keep a good man down, his job has expanded – as has the railway. An extra mile of track has been laid – with the help of a Youth Opportunities Scheme – and now he is busy working out budgets and projected cash flow for the coming twelve months.

REACH
Victoria House,
Southampton Row,
London WC1B 4DH.   phone: 01-404-0940

Further reading:
REACH, *Work After Work*, (Quiller Press, 1984), £2.95.

The enormous range of voluntary work now available means that there will certainly be something to suit you. But obviously you must sit down and think a little about your needs too. It is bad enough doing a paid job that you hate; it would be silly to get yourself involved with voluntary work that you do not enjoy. Do you like organizing other people? Or being pointed in the direction you can be of most help? Does the idea of being part of a team appeal or would you rather find a way of making your contribution on your own? Do you find young people irritating or would you welcome the opportunity of mixing with a different age group?

THE NATIONAL COUNCIL FOR VOLUNTARY ORGANIZATIONS

The National Council publishes a complete list of voluntary groups – classified by subject. It costs £4.50, but you should be able to have a look at a copy in your local library (and make a note of the organizations of special interest).

The National Council for Voluntary
Organizations,
26 Bedford Square,
London WC1.   phone: 01-636-4066

Further reading: *Voluntary Organizations*, published by NCVO.

VOLUNTEER CENTRES

Many towns now have a Volunteer Centre, where they will be able to advise you on volunteering opportunities that are available locally. If there is no centre near you, your local Citizens' Advice Bureau will be only too pleased to hear from you, or you could contact:

Volunteer Centre,
29 Lower King's Road,
Berkhamstead,
Hertfordshire.   phone: 04427-73311

If you have been looking forward to your retirement because it will enable you to do some travelling abroad, there are two voluntary organizations which might be able to help.

BRITISH EXECUTIVE SERVICE OVERSEAS (BESO)

This is an independent organization initiated by the Institute of Directors, with government help. They send experienced businessmen with management, professional or technical skills to advise small- and medium-sized businesses in developing countries.

Assignments last a maximum of six months, the average three to four months. Although you do not receive a salary, BESO will pay for air travel (for you and your partner), a clothing allowance and weekly expenses of around £25. In addition, accommodation, subsistence and local transport are provided by the country you visit. Which country you visit will obviously depend on what skills you have to offer and where they are most needed. You must be fit, of course, but the upper age limit on these trips has now been raised to seventy years of age.

Stephen Bull, who is now sixty-six, worked at Hotpoint in Peterborough as a tooling manager for many years. In February 1983, he went to Kingston, Jamaica, at the request of the Jamaica Industrial Development Corporation. The Corporation was looking for help and advice in setting up a comprehensive training programme for their instructors. Mr Bull undertook the assignment and it was successfully completed in just under six months.

British Executive Service Overseas,
116-119 Pall Mall,
London SW1Y 5ED.   phone: 01-839-1233

VOLUNTARY SERVICE OVERSEAS (VSO)

When VSO was formed, over twenty years ago, it was largely intrepid youngsters, often with a year to kill before going to university, who set off to remote places to 'help out'. It is now recognized that professional skills are equally needed, and out of the 600 or so volunteers that go abroad each year, at least sixty are likely to be retired people. Most projects last for a period of two years, and the upper age limit at VSO is sixty-five (which means you would be returning at sixty-seven). The range of opportunities is very large: librarians, accountants, self-employed businessmen and many more. If you want to take your partner you need to volunteer as a couple. As with BESO, travel, accommodation and expenses are paid.

Voluntary Service Overseas,
9 Belgrave Square,
London SW1.   phone: 01-235-5191

If the idea appeals, but you are worried about dipping into your savings to keep up payments at home for rates, insurance and so on, remember that you may be able to let your house or flat on a short lease while you are away.

COMMUNITY SERVICE VOLUNTEERS

This is the sister organization to VSO, with branches throughout Britain. Much of their work involves young people, which is why they are very keen to have more mature people on hand to help and advise.

Community Service Volunteers,
237 Pentonville Road,
London N1.   phone: 01-278-6601

There are many organizations and services, such as meals on wheels, that depend on voluntary help. Those who want to become involved in some type of work, but who don't want paid employment, may find that helping one of these organizations is the ideal solution.

The number of organizations needing help now runs well into four figures and it is difficult to mention some whilst omitting others. All of them will be delighted to hear from you and to explain more about their work. There are three more publications which give you specific details of the sort of work available:

Gundry, E. *Sparing Time, The Observer Guide to Helping Others*, (Unwin, 1981), £2.25.
Gundry, E. *Helping Hands, A Guide to Conservation* (Unwin, 1981), £2.25.
Have You Heard? Help The Aged, Education Department, 60p.

So far we have mentioned only organized voluntary work. Chances are you already know somebody looking after a housebound or frail relative. The cut-backs in social services in most areas have created a situation where many people nowadays carry a heavy burden of responsibility, with very little help for providing round-the-clock nursing care. A few hours break, while you 'sit' for them, can make a huge difference. Even the opportunity to do some leisurely shopping or enjoy a cup of coffee out, with the pressure off, can totally change a person's life; and it is not exaggerating to say that in some cases these brief respites are the only thing that stands between the 'carer' and a nervous breakdown.

Self-employment

Kay Sykes

Many people think that retirement is the perfect time to set up something new, on their own or with a friend. Do think long and hard about it first. For a start, all work, however invigorating, is also tiring. If you take on short-term paid or voluntary work you can always take a long break, or stop altogether if it becomes too much. This is much more difficult if you are running your own business. Anyone who has worked for a small company will agree that the strain on the person running it can be enormous, however successful the business is.

And if the idea of opening up a shop is alluring because you could please yourself, after years of trying to fit in with your employer's wishes, you are in for a big shock. The tact and flexibility needed to be a good employee are required in even *greater* measure if you are dealing with suppliers and customers.

For those who enter retirement with a lump sum from their previous employer the advice is, proceed with caution! Partnerships, franchises and suchlike often need far more capital than they suggest and, sadly, there is no 'Get Rich Quick' recipe for success; there is no room, either, for amateurs in business these days.

On the positive side, if you are determined to go ahead, there is help at hand. There are two government sponsored organizations with representatives throughout the country.

Small Firms Advisory Service, (run by the Department of Industry)
Ebury Bridge House,
Ebury Bridge Road,
London SW1.   phone: Freephone 2444

COSIRA: Council for Small Industries in Rural Areas,
141 Castle Street,
Salisbury,
Wiltshire.   phone: Salisbury (0722) 336255

Franchises, as we mentioned earlier, can run into enormous problems. If you are serious, make sure you talk to several other franchisees and ask them if their results have lived up to expectations, and how many hours they have had to put in to achieve their turnover. Check the small print *very carefully*, and see what provision there is to sell back your franchise. Make sure you get good legal advice, and do not sign anything without consulting your solicitor and bank manager. Also there to help:

The British Franchise Association,
15 The Poynings,
Iver,
Buckinghamshire.   phone: Iver (0753) 653546

Your local Chamber of Trade will also be able to advise you and you can contact them through:

The National Chamber of Trade,
Enterprise House,
Henley-on-Thames,
Oxon RG9 1TU.

Scottish Retail Federation,
203 Pitt Street,
Glasgow G2 7JG.

For those who do not want the responsibility of running a full-time business, but who would like a little extra money, there are other opportunities.

Mail order companies These will pay you a small commission on any items you sell from their catalogues. Look for advertisements in the daily press.

Home selling You can become a representative for a particular company, who will advise you how to sell their goods; either through selling 'parties', or by visiting people in their homes who have already expressed an interest in the product.

Direct Selling Association,
44 Russell Square,
London WC1B 4JP.   phone: 01-580-8433

Private tuition This is a possibility if you are a retired teacher, or have a special skill, such as fluency in another language, or if you are an accomplished musician. Your best bet is to put an advertisement in the local newsagents.

Garden produce and home cooked food You can sell garden produce straight from your door, once you have permission from the local council. Or

you could join the Women's Institute Co-Operative Market Scheme.

The Market Adviser,
National Federation of Women's Institutes,
39 Eccleston Street,
London SW1 9NL.   phone: 01-730-7212
(She will tell you the address of your nearest branch)

And if you enjoy cooking, *Food As Presents* (P. H. White, Penguin, 1982) has plenty of excellent recipes and suggestions for packing your produce to make it look attractive.

There are now thousands of 'one-man' bands dotted all over Britain, enjoying the flexibility of working in their own time.

One word of warning: if you need a workshop

This group of pensioners got together to grow vegetables. If you have a surplus of home-produced vegetables and fruit, you can sell them at your door or gate provided that you have obtained permission from the council.

or are going in for something which might cause public disquiet (e.g., setting up kennels or a cattery) do make sure you have the necessary licences and planning permission.

Although none of these activities will make you a fortune, they can be very rewarding to the individual.

Education

Perhaps the idea of spending the weekend in a beautiful country house, enjoying good food and interesting conversation, and learning about bridge or photography, is pretty far removed from your idea of 'education'? In fact, it is just one of the many opportunities that now exist, because the whole concept of education has changed so dramatically over the last fifty years.

Retirement certainly offers the ideal opportunity to explore areas that you have always wanted to discover, but have never had the time for. Now there is such a wealth of different types of classes available, it is quite difficult to know where to start.

Close to home . . . .

LOCAL EDUCATION CLASSES

The best known classes are those organized by local authorities. Most of these are geared to people who have had little formal education and in many cases they hold different levels of classes for some subjects, for example, French for Beginners, Advanced Needlework. Part-time day and evening classes run by local authorities are open to *all* adults, not just retired people. Often the different age groups and occupations of

Local authority day and evening classes provide the opportunity to learn a new subject or skill in a relaxed and friendly atmosphere. Some councils offer greatly reduced rates to retired people, but this will depend on the area in which you live.

the students provide as much interest and enjoyment as the classes themselves. The subjects, too, vary enormously. Everything you can think of, from anthropology, antiques, art and astronomy to woodwork and writing, yoga and zoology.

Of course, some local authority classes *do* have older people especially in mind. Keep Fit for the Over-Fifties, for example, or Cook and Eat groups aimed primarily at that age group. Old Time Dancing might fall into that category, or classes dealing with Oral History, that is, history that can best be described by people who have actually lived through it. Each local authority has an adult education service, often organized into an Adult Education Institute. They are the people to contact if you want to find out more about classes in your area. Alternatively, your local library will have the details.

You may find there are no existing classes that correspond to your particular area of interest. But if you do have a passionate enthusiasm for a special subject – Chinese Cooking, for instance, or Roman History – and if you can find a number of people who share your interest, there is nothing to stop you approaching the principal of your local education institute and asking him to provide a course. If you are going to do this, it is quite important to make sure that you really have the support and commitment of the people who are interested, as most local authorities will cancel courses if they are not well attended; for example, if there are fewer than ten students over a three-week period.

Some councils offer greatly reduced rates to retired people. For instance, Liverpool's adult education classes are free to pensioners. Those living in Inner London pay only £1 a year for any number of classes, any number of courses.

The full cost of classes varies depending on your local authority. £12, for example, would pay for a twenty-eight-week course in the London Borough of Bromley, or one term of ten two-hour classes in Hereford and Worcester. If you feel that concessionary rates for retired people are inadequate in your area, it may be worthwhile complaining to your local authority. If they feel there is pressure for a reduction – and a demand from pensioners for courses – it could

make sense for them to broaden their concessionary rates.

Even with the cut-backs we have seen in recent years, and the rise in the cost of fees, local education classes are still a bargain. Most adult education institutes have some classes in the daytime. The choice of subjects may be more limited, but you do not have to go out and return in the dark. In addition, if you spend a day doing, say, chair upholstery in a class, you are not using up gas or electricity at home, so your bills should be less.

Your local education authority or local library will have details.

WORKERS' EDUCATION ASSOCIATION (WEA)

Despite its rather austere title, this is a non-political organization which has approximately 170,000 members attending a variety of day and evening classes, in subjects as varied as politics, human relations and sociology. Each group has a degree of autonomy, so the classes offered vary from one area to another. You can start your own course by getting together with other people who have similar interests. WEA's district offices are always responsive to a demand for a new course, provided that at least fifteen people want it. The WEA offer a 50 per cent reduction on fees to retired people. They also organize a number of summer schools and study tours, both in Britain and abroad.

When *Years Ahead* first mentioned the WEA on the programme, Joan Willcock from Warsash in Hampshire was just one of the many viewers who made the point: 'I know WEA sounds as if it has political overtones – it doesn't'.

Mrs Willcock had nothing but praise, too, for the WEA summer schools – combined holiday/education courses: 'Like many women whose families are adult, I find that "interest holidays" are the perfect answer – lots of fascinating things to learn all day, with good food, good company and evening visits to theatres, concerts, etc.'

The Workers' Education Association,
9 Upper Berkeley Street,
London W1H 8BY.   phone: 01-402-5608

Away from home . . . .
NATIONAL INSTITUTE OF CONTINUING ADULT EDUCATION

For those who like the idea of a weekend away from home that is educational as well as enjoyable, the National Institute of Adult Education co-ordinates a number of what they call 'Residential Short Courses' nationwide. Most courses last for a weekend; you stay at universities, or at houses and halls in the country. These courses are also open to *all* adults, and they tend not to be too academic. The choice of subjects is staggering. Everything from chess, pottery, embroidery or tracing your ancestors, to an examination of Rodgers and Hart musicals! They also include classes such as rambling, that are likely to find a greater response among the older age group. Courses last a weekend, a week, or even several weeks. An average weekend course costs about £30. They are very popular because they combine short breaks from everyday routine, with opportunities to learn more about a particular subject and meet new people and exchange fresh ideas. The National Institute of Continuing Adult Education publishes a calendar of events, twice yearly, in January and August, covering a six-month schedule.

The National Institute of Continuing Adult Education,
19B De Montfort Street,
Leicester LE1 7GE.   phone: 0533 551451

FIELD STUDY CENTRES

If you are a nature lover, or like the idea of learning more about the countryside, then the Field Study Centres may be for you.

There are ten centres in England and Wales, offering an extraordinarily diverse range of subjects: Suffolk churches, wild flowers for beginners, nature photography and wine-making are just a few. Their short residential courses are often held in large country houses. The centre at Preston also has facilities for the disabled and special courses 'for those not entirely agile'.

Field Studies Council,
Preston,
Montford,
Shrewsbury.

FURTHER EDUCATION IN UNIVERSITIES AND POLYTECHNICS

Many colleges, schools and universities are now opening their doors to older students, and offering a wide variety of courses to people who may have left school over fifty years ago.

Attending a college as a full-time student may seem a daunting prospect if you are retired. But there are now 'taster' courses lasting a few days, designed to give older people an idea of what academic study can be like. In North London, for instance, the Middlesex Polytechnic organizes a five-day 'Return to Learning' course every September, for older people only. There they can judge what sort of subjects they might find appealing, or whether the whole idea is, after all, not really for them. This course costs about £40 to resident students, but only £9 if you arrange your own accommodation during the week. There are seventy places on the course, and students come from all over the country to take subjects ranging from environmental studies to philosophy and theories of history.

If the whole idea of academic activity appeals to you, you can go on to study for a degree, full-time or part-time, working and studying alongside younger students.

There are, in fact, an increasing number of polytechnics and universities that offer what they call 'open admissions' policies towards older students, allowing them to study for a degree at their own pace, and without requiring from them formal qualifications like GCEs, and so on. Leeds and Hatfield Polytechnics were among the pioneers in this area, the University of Lancaster another. There are now twenty-one universities offering similar possibilities, so it is worth enquiring at your nearest polytechnic or university.

The Directory of Further Education, *The Comprehensive Guide to Courses in UK Polytechnics and Colleges*, is available at your local reference library.

Ted Goodfriend's favourite subject at school was history, but he says that when he left at eighteen the idea of further education did not really occur to him. Instead he took up another career, which spanned fifty-four years, ending up as sales director of a perfume company. But in summer, 1982, Ted spotted a tiny piece in the local paper about the 'Return to Learning' course at Middlesex Polytechnic. When he enrolled, Ted was amazed at how helpful everyone was and how much he enjoyed both exchanging new ideas, and the social aspect of the course. Stimulated by this success, Ted decided to embark on a full-time degree course at Middlesex, where he is reading Humanities. Ted is now in his second year – and anxious to share the credit for his achievement with his wife, Sally, without whom, he says, he could never have done it. An interesting bonus for Ted has been a greater understanding of the younger students with whom he works. 'It's too easy', he says, 'if you're sitting at home, cut off from the younger generation, to get a rather warped view of them. Studying alongside them day after day you begin to understand things better from their point of view.' Ted is far too modest to mention the enormous contribution he has no doubt made to *their* studies!

OPEN UNIVERSITY

Another very different way of studying for a degree is with the Open University. Courses are based on broadcast television lectures. You study for an Open University degree at home, and send your essays and written work through the post to your tutor. About one in eight of all Open University graduates are over sixty. Many of them have had no formal education. Most people will already have come across at least part of a broadcast from the Open University when switching from one television channel to another. If you like the idea of studying at home, all the Open University time-tables are published in the *Radio Times* and some of the daily newspapers. Why not select a few programmes and watch them, and then send away for more details.

The Open University is not just for people who want to obtain a degree. They also have an Associate Student Programme. This consists of nearly 200 'pack' courses: you receive written information and an audio or video cassette through the post. This way you can learn on your own, or, even better, get together with a group of people who share your interest. If you learn together, you have the added bonus of sharing your experience with others and getting the benefit of an exchange of views.

With these courses, which cover a wide variety of topics – from jazz to planning your retirement – you do not send away 'homework' for assessment. But there will be a local coordinator in the area who can advise you if you want further help. The Open University short courses are specially designed for 'people who want a challenge, but not a degree'.

The Open University,
Walton Hall,
Milton Keynes MK7 6AA.　　　　phone: 0908 653791

CORRESPONDENCE COURSES

If you like the idea of working from home, but you do want written assessment of your work, then why not try a correspondence course?

The National Extension College have a number of courses specially prepared for adults who left school at fifteen or sixteen years of age, and have not done any studying since. And they give specially reduced rates to people of retirement age.

If you find an advertisement for a correspondence course that interests you, but you are not sure about the quality of the tuition, enquire about it to the Council for the Accreditation of Correspondence Colleges, a watch-dog body which regularly checks the standards of the various colleges.

National Extension College,
18 Brooklands Avenue,
Cambridge CB2 2HN.

Council for the Accreditation of Correspondence Colleges,
27 Marylebone Road,
London NW1 5JS.　　　　phone: 01-935-5391

UNIVERSITY OF THE THIRD AGE

One of the most interesting developments in recent years is the emergence of the University of the Third Age (U3A), specially designed for older people. The concept, taken from France, is that of a network of self-help groups, whereby people educate themselves by sharing their experience and knowledge. Not only do the groups avoid the strains of competitive exams and diplomas, but they also try to do away with the whole idea of teacher-pupil relationships. So much so, that the original visionary aim was that of a generalized exchange of skills, interest and experience, without any formal curriculum at all. Most groups in this country have found that they function best with some organized classes and fairly traditional subjects such as French, English, Art History and so on. The point is that the members themselves decide on the curriculum, and do their own administration. Each group, therefore, has a great deal of autonomy and can decide how much to charge to cover administrative costs.

The national office in London co-ordinates the various groups, and serves as a central contact point for further information. At present there are about thirty U3A groups around the country. The U3A National Committee office will be able to tell you if there is a group near you, or they will send you an information pack, on request, which gives helpful advice on how to set up your own group in your area.

University of the Third Age,
National Committee,
6 Parkside Gardens,
London SW19 5EY.   phone: 01-947-0401

'SOUNDS OKAY, BUT NOT FOR ME . . .'

If you have read through all the possibilities outlined here and come to the conclusion: 'They sound interesting, but I'd never be able to cope . . .' *think again!*

One of the convenient myths of old age is that

Ted Goodfriend (third from right) is studying for a degree in Humanities at Middlesex Polytechnic. In addition to enjoying his studies, Ted appreciates the opportunity to work alongside younger students.

the brain no longer works as well as it used to. Yet when Sir Winston Churchill became Prime Minister in 1940 (after his years in the 'wilderness') no-one objected on the grounds that his brain was 'rusty'. Yet he was sixty-six. Mao Tse Tung was fifty-six when he took power in China. He ruled until his death at the age of eighty-two.

It is possible to quote plenty of favourable statistics, too, comparing the study results of people over sixty with those of younger students. However, it is not the statistics that matter here; more important is what *you* believe you can or cannot do.

If you are still feeling nervous about the idea of taking up classes, look back for a moment at your own, perhaps hated, schooldays. No matter how much you may have loathed school, there was almost certainly one subject you liked. Probably it was one you also did well in – and that is just the important point here. Nobody is going to expect you to study algebra (or whatever it was you hated). Now is the time to concentrate on doing whatever it was you *enjoyed*.

If you are still hesitating, why not ease yourself back in the water – gently – by enrolling for just one term in a subject you already know quite a bit about, something practical perhaps? When you have got your confidence back you can go on to tackle Advanced Ancient Greek, or whatever else interests you.

There is an excellent book on the subject of how to make studying easier. It is called *Use Your Head* by Tony Buzan, (BBC Publications), £3.95.

Many commercial holiday companies and organizations such as the National Trust now combine straightforward holidays with tuition of some kind.

For further information see also the section on Holidays, page 30.

Hobbies

Everyone, the 'retirement specialists' agree, should have a hobby. But what exactly constitutes a hobby these days? How do you categorize a week's residential course in a country house

Arthur Reece considered that knitting was an 'old woman's hobby' until he retired at the age of seventy and invested in a knitting machine. In the following four months, he made fifty jumpers, and sold all but this one.

learning about creative writing? Is it a holiday, education or a hobby? It is, of course, all three, which is why you will find plenty of suggestions for pursuing hobbies in those particular sections of this book. Almost everyone has taken up a hobby at some point in their lives and this may well be the ideal time to pursue it further. Or you may prefer to embark on something completely new, connected perhaps with your previous employment.

Percy Phillips lives in Bristol. When he retired from his job as a metal worker, he started making flowers out of empty beer cans. He had seen some flowers made out of wood and was struck by how 'flat' they looked. He felt sure that by making them out of metal, so that he could bend the 'petals' into shape, they would look more life-like. He has been very successful: his beer-can flowers are popular presents, and he has even sold some. And of course it is an inexpensive hobby – people are only too pleased to find a good home for their empty beer cans.

Collecting has become very popular over the last decade or so. Again, it does not have to be expensive, unless you decide on Ming jars or something similar.

Harry Chew was an avid coin collector for many years, until one day he was passing a skip and happened to notice some old locks and keys. The locks were broken, but he took the keys and his collection began.

He now has some 400 to 500 keys and has become very knowledgeable about them. His oldest key, used for the lock on a panier – the type that used to be slung over a horse's back - – cost just 75p. He has become something of a local celebrity because his advice is always being sought by people who have acquired old chests and cannot find keys to fit the locks.

There seemed a very real danger some years ago that many of our ancient skills and pastimes would die out, through lack of interest. That situation has now changed, with the younger generation showing an avid interest in the old-fashioned way of doing things – but of course they still need someone to teach them.

Take bell-ringing, for instance. You are never too old to start, according to Geoffrey Hemming of Evesham, Worcester, and he should know – he is in his eighties. He likes it because it brings him into contact with other people of all ages.

Central Council of Church Bell Ringers,
Penmark House,
Guildford,
Surrey.

Whatever your particular interest, it pays to be bold, to go for the impossible, because you just never know . . . .

Edna Mainwaring lives in North Wales and has been keen on bowls all her life. Her wild, impossible dream? To play on the Waterloo Green in Blackpool, the Wembley of bowling. She began to organize a 'Granny Bowling Competition' at her local club. Then, taking her courage in both hands, Edna rang the administrators at the Waterloo Gardens and they agreed to let her have the green. She got some sponsorship from the local paper, and then wrote to *Years Ahead* asking if any of the viewers would like to attend. *Years Ahead* filmed the competition for the programme, and a great success it was too.

Competitors taking part in the 'Granny Bowling Competition' which Edna Mainwaring organized at the Waterloo Green in Blackpool.

It is possible, too, to be a 'collector' without actually buying or hoarding anything.

> Fred Fuzzens collects pillar-boxes, or rather pictures of the unusual ones. Fred first became interested when he spotted an old Victorian pillar-box, and from then on he started looking out for them. Whenever he and his wife go away on holiday Fred cannot pass a pillar-box without checking to see if it is a type he has not come across before.

There is such a huge choice of hobbies, and so many books have already been written on the subject, that it is impossible to list them all here, but this is where your local library is useful. On their notice-boards, they usually post details of the classes, groups or exhibitions taking place in the area. They will also have many books on the subject. Remember, too, that if you hear about a new book but feel it is too expensive to buy, they will often get a copy for you.

Materials can sometimes prove a problem if your hobby is, say, painting, but in all likelihood your children, grandchildren and the rest of the family will be only too pleased to know their birthday and Christmas present problems are solved from now on: they can always find some-thing to suit, from a new easel, to a bottle of turps.

Some hobbies can be quite lucrative, or at least useful. If you are making something to sell, start off in a small way, but do not underestimate the time and effort (and materials) you have put into it by selling too cheaply. If you hope to make money, think carefully before committing yourself to any major outlay. Animal breeding, for instance, could be a possibility, but do get advice from the experts. Bee-keeping is another option, and the excess honey should not be difficult to sell.

A monthly magazine called *Popular Crafts* is very useful for anyone interested in arts and crafts (price 60p), and they have now published an excellent book called *Popular Crafts Guide to Good Craft Suppliers*. It contains details of hundreds of suppliers, cross-referenced by area and subject.

Barrett, E. & Fogden, L. *Popular Crafts Guide to Good Craft Suppliers*, (Argus Books, 1983), £1.75.

Family history

Jack Amos, seventy-six-year-old grandfather, wondered on what day of the week he had been born. From his retirement home in East Anglia, he travelled to London and visited the Guildhall Library where, he had been told, there are copies of the daily *Times* from the date it was first printed. The Librarian brought him a bound volume of *The Times*, which included the copy for May 23rd 1903, the day of his birth. It was a Saturday: Issue No. 37088, twenty-two pages at 3 pence!

Told he could stay until 5 pm, Jack sat engrossed in creating a picture of the world of his childhood. Being a pensioner, he was particularly interested in the report of the second reading of the Bill for the provision of pensions for the aged deserving poor, which proposed that at the age of sixty-five a pension should be paid, of not less than 5 shillings, and not more than 7 shillings. He also looked at the property pages: a country mansion offered at £4,500, comprising a billiard

One of the aspects of retirement that many people particularly look forward to is the opportunity to spend more time on their hobbies. And for some people, what was a hobby can become a reliable new source of income.

room, twenty bed- and dressing-rooms, a paddock with 9½ acres, and wonderful views of the South Downs! Other items caught his eye: a motor car, a Renault 4½ hp to seat four for £160; and a £9.19.6 cruise to Norway.

It has been estimted that a copy of *The Times* contains as much information as the average book. If that is true, then considering that in Britain today some 7,000 newspapers and magazines are published and that the first newspaper appeared in the seventeenth century, the total amount of information on people and events published during the past 300 years must be staggering.

His interest now thoroughly aroused, Jack decided to return to the scene of his childhood at Clapham Common, London, and trace old friends, his church, home and school, and other remembered haunts, some of which had disappeared in the World War II bombing and redevelopment.

This was four years ago, and with his talent for drawing, Jack has produced a written and illustrated 'history', which is a treasured possession of his children and grandchildren.

Jack, as a late child and youngest of ten children, can jump back 100 years in two generations! When we consider that the parents of today's teenagers may well not have been born until the war years of the 1940s, it is a timely reminder that all our memories are history – a very personal family and social history.

Perhaps you have no family of your own. Nevertheless you may be able to provide a personal account of experience in the war years, or of a locality as it was fifty years ago, or a place of work. Any of these could be a welcome addition to a local history collection or record office, or

Jack Amos's interest in family history began when he decided to find out on what day of the week he was born. From that he went on to trace his friends, home and school, and remembered haunts. In all, he spent four years researching, writing and illustrating his own history.

Association of British Craftsmen,
57 Coombe Bridge Avenue,
Bristol.

The English Tourist Board publishes a marvellous booklet, entitled *Activity and Hobby Holidays in England*, price £1.25, giving details of hundreds of activity holidays. They also provide information about other holidays in England, particularly cheap weekend breaks, in *Let's Go* (free).

English Tourist Board,
4 Grosvenor Gardens,
London SW1.   phone: 01-730-3400

One reason many people hesitate to take their holidays in Britain is the weather. But not all holidays actually *need* good weather for you to enjoy them. Two favourites with our own Ethel Chipchase (see page 86) are canal and rambling holidays. On a canal holiday the barges usually travel in pairs (with about six guests on each boat), mooring overnight (often near a pub!). This way you enjoy the local countryside, strolling along the tow path, helping to open and close the locks as you go through. And with rambling, once you have invested in some weatherproof clothing, the costs, whether for a day out or a whole week, are fairly low.

For the even more energetic, the YMCA have adventure holidays in the Lake District where activities include sailing, rock climbing, archery and environmental studies. A week here will cost about £100.

Inland Waterways Holiday Cruises Ltd,
Preston Brook,
Cheshire WA7 3AL.   phone: (09286) 376
or (0606) 852405

British Waterways Board,
Melbury House,
Melbury Terrace,
London NW1 6JX.   phone: 01-262-6711

Holiday Fellowship Holidays Ltd, (rambling)
142-144 Great North Way,
London NW4 1EG.   phone: 01-203-6711

Ramblers' Association,
1-5 Wandsworth Road,
London SW8 2LJ.   phone: 01-582-6878

YMCA National Centre,
Lakeside,
Ulverston,
Cumbria LA12 8BD.   phone: 0448 31758

There are now several companies who offer reduced rates and special holidays for retired people. Of these, the best known is probably SAGA. If you are dreading the dismal prospect of a cold British winter (with hideously high fuel bills) you might be interested to know that last winter SAGA were offering a three-and-a-half month holiday (sixteen weeks) in Fuengirola, Southern Spain, in a pleasant hotel *with full board* for £666.61. At just over £40 a week it really can be cheaper than staying at home. They have also come up with some other interesting ideas such as 'Only Ones' for single pensioners where you will not feel left out because you are not part of a 'couple', and 'Ruby Wedding Holidays' which

Several companies organize special holidays at reduced rates for retired people, and these can be an ideal way to escape the British winter. Whether you want to spend two weeks enjoying the sunshine in Spain, or to go for something adventurous, you are sure to find a holiday that would suit you from the wide variety available.

includes a simple, but moving, church ceremony in which you renew your wedding vows, followed by a party and champagne.

It would be totally wrong to assume that SAGA holidays are only for the very old and decrepit. Last year they had a three-week holiday based in Delhi, India, which included lots of interesting excursions, including two days in Katmandu. Certainly not something for the faint-hearted!

SAGA, of course, is only one of the many travel companies offering special holidays and your local travel agent should have plenty of brochures to show you.

SAGA
119 Sandgate Road,
Folkestone,
Kent CT20 2BN.   phone: Folkestone
(0303) 30000

Raymond Cook Holidays have been going for over fifty years, providing 'holidays for Christian folk'. They cover the Oberammergau Passion Play, the Holy Land, as well as a wide selection of other destinations, most of them with an escort or 'leader' who will make sure you are able to attend Sunday worship (for those who wish to) and ensure that anyone travelling alone does not feel left out.

Raymond Cook Holidays,
118 High Street,
Dover,
Kent CT16 1ED. phone: Dover (0304) 204404
or 203607

There are two other ways of escaping the British winter. One way is by *villa-sitting*, which means acting as a guardian in a Mediterranean villa for which you pay a truly nominal rent. Retired people are much in demand because it is assumed (I wonder if correctly?) they will not be having wild parties every night.

Mediterranean Properties,
Whitworth Chambers,
George Row,
Northampton,
Northants NN1 1DF.   phone: (0604) 20404

Or check *The Lady* for small ads.

Another option is *Home Interchange Limited*. For a subscription of £16.50 you receive two issues of the *Exchange Book*, which includes names, addresses and details of properties available for swapping all over the world (including, of course, your own entry). Not only do you save money on the 'extras' you would incur in a hotel, but also you know that your home is that much more secure while you are away.

Home Interchange Limited,
8 Hillside,
Farningham,
Kent DA4 ODD.   phone (0322) 864527

If you are thinking of moving abroad, or even to another part of the country, this is the way to get to know the area under 'normal' conditions.

If you have relatives or friends on the other side of the world, and the only thing holding you back from visiting them is the picture of yourself stranded in a foreign airport somewhere – with no idea which plane you should be getting on – the answer is a Reunion Club. In addition to discounts on the actual fare, they will take care of you from the moment you start your journey, until you fall into the arms of your family.

British Airways Reunion Clubs,
PO Box 13,
Victoria Terminal,
Buckingham Palace Road,
London SW1W 9SR.   phone: 01-821-4631

For many people retirement is the time they think about visiting the grave of a father or brother lost during the two world wars. Other ex-servicemen and women simply hanker to go back to see if it is all as they remembered. A number of companies now offer these trips; one of them, Holt's, say they use the coach journey as a 'time capsule' taking the traveller back to the period with the use of contemporary literature, magazines, sounds and slides.

Major and Mrs Holt's Battlefield Tours,
Oak House,
Woodnesborough,
Sandwich,
Kent.   phone: Sandwich (0304) 612248

Glenton Tours,
114 Peckham Rye,
London SE15 4JE.   phone: 01-639-9777

Townsend Thorensen,
Enterprise House,
Avebury Avenue,
Tunbridge Wells,
Kent.

For other holiday offers, such as Railcards, see also the section on Bargains: page 47.

When planning your holiday do compare prices offered by different companies. The costs can vary enormously and the savings to be made by going either one week earlier or later can make quite a difference. Some tour operators also offer three weeks for the price of two at certain times of the year and although many people obviously have a 'brand' loyalty it really does pay to shop around.

Lastly, do make sure you have adequate insurance – and read the small print to see exactly what it covers. For example £1000 may seem plenty for medical expenses, but it certainly will not go far if you have a heart attack in the United States – the size of the bill could be enough to bring one on! Apart from that: Bon Voyage . . . .

Pets

Bill Wadman-Taylor

In recent years, various scientific studies have been made into the keeping of pets – which scientists call 'companion animals' to be more precise. These have demonstrated statistically that people with certain illnesses – particularly heart conditions – have a better survival rate if they are pet owners. In the field of psychology, scientists are telling us what many of us have always known: that the two-way communication between human and pet, the reciprocated appreciation and demonstration of affection, is conducive to peace of mind and therefore a relaxed and balanced mentality. Most of the tests have been

Bill Wadman-Taylor (left).

done with furry pets, the ones which invite stroking. But the satisfaction of talking to a cage bird, or watching gliding fish in a tank should not be underestimated.

Devotion to a pet is often thought of as a substitute for devotion to family or other humans. Frequently it is; when children have grown up and left home, and in cases of bereavement, it may be the only alternative. In such cases the pet is a very valuable asset and provides one of the basic human requirements: companionship. But equally often pet-loving goes on side by side with normal family life; indeed, children and pets often have a unique relationship.

Before choosing a pet, examine your own disposition. If you take the view that a pet will add unnecessarily to the household chores and be a nuisance, you should go for one of the less demanding options. On the other hand, if you are the sort of person who gets pleasure from doing things for others, then you will enjoy lavishing the love and attention a young puppy needs.

Before making your decision on what sort of pet to have, there are three other points you should consider: purse and premises, preference, and patience. Let us deal with them in turn.

PURSE AND PREMISES
How much can you afford, or how much do you wish to spend? Of the usual pets, dogs are the most expensive. A pedigree puppy is not likely to cost less than about £50 and some of the rarer breeds are very much more. Incidentally, it is usually worth buying a pedigree puppy because you know how it is going to turn out as regards size and appearance. If you get a puppy of unknown parentage, it may grow up to be very different from the sort of dog you like, or it may turn out to be an unsuitable size for your house. A pedigree dog costs no more to feed than a mongrel, but the cost will vary with size; obviously a large dog will eat more than a small one. Some dogs, such as poodles, also require periodic trimming, and this adds to the expense.

Kittens come next on the list; they are usually very inexpensive or even free, unless you want one of the more exotic pure-breds. Cats are relatively cheap to feed and are catholic in their

You may decide to keep a pet for the sake of companionship. However, many people get a great deal of pleasure and satisfaction from entering their pets in shows at local and national level.

tastes – unless you allow them to become too fussy. It is a myth that cats eat only fish. The coats of some long-haired breeds need de-matting occasionally, and this can be an unexpected addition to your expenses.

Cage birds vary in price according to their rarity. Cages and ancillary equipment must be added to the cost. But once this initial expenditure is over, cage birds cost very little to feed and, barring illness, they need no attention that will cost money.

Fish can be very cheap to buy: from about 30p upwards. They are also cheap to feed, but a moderately-sized tank and the equipment to go with it will cost about £30 to £50.

PREFERENCE
This must be considered in conjunction with purse and premises. You may prefer a St Bernard dog to any other pet, but if you are of small stature, or live in a small house with lots of knick-knacks and little ornaments on low tables, such a dog would be more of a pest than a pet. Most large dogs are expensive to buy and feed and need expert rearing and a lot of exercise. Thus such a dog may be more than a pet, it can be a serious hobby and require a lot of study and attention. Definitely not for the beginner but an absorbing, almost full-time occupation for anyone with suitable accommodation and adequate income.

Do not think that small dogs are less intelligent, or have less character than big dogs. There are so many small dogs to choose from, and in general their character depends on how they are brought up.

Cats will fit in almost anywhere – from a croft to a castle. Although they are more independent than dogs, they do respond in their own way to human affection. The purr of a contented cat is a wonderfully soothing, satisfying sound that no dog can emulate. Cats do not need to be house-trained as they are usually naturally clean from a very early age; they groom themselves, too. On average they live longer than dogs: many cats live to seventeen or even twenty. In general, they are less prone to disease than dogs and, with luck, the only veterinary fee you will have to meet is that for having the cat neutered.

Cage birds and aquarium fish do not take up much space and they take their own exercise. Many people find them very absorbing pets – witness the numbers that are sold each year – and they are certainly decorative. The commonest cage bird is the budgerigar, but there are others, such as parrots, macaws and minah birds. Canaries have become less common in recent years but are very attractive, though of course they do not talk like parrots and budgies, and only the males sing.

Fish fall into two main categories: coldwater and tropical. Both include some very beautiful and quite cheap specimens that are easy to look after. The tropical varieties need a constantly heated tank, but there are many inexpensive heaters on the market which work automatically.

PATIENCE

This applies mainly to rearing and training young puppies, but to a lesser extent to nearly all pets. All dogs demand some attention from you: feeding, most need cleaning and grooming, bed-changing, and so on, and your watchful eye on their welfare. In return, you will have the pleasure of a likeable and well-behaved companion. Adult dogs always reflect the upbringing they have had, so you may be judged by your dog's behaviour!

I have not dealt with the more unusual pets, such as white mice, rats, gerbils, hamsters, monkeys, and so on. I would strongly urge anyone contemplating keeping any of these to get expert information and advice before taking any action.

If none of the pets mentioned appeals to you, there is one other possibility: why not make a 'pet' of a local wild animal? I know a lady who puts food out for a hedgehog. It comes at the same time each day for its meals and shows no fear of her or her bulldog. A word of warning, though. Putting out food in the garden may attract unwanted pets, such as rats and foxes.

Undoubtedly, birds are the most rewarding wild pets. A little studying and experimenting will reveal which foods attract which species; what time of day they like to eat; how their demands vary with the weather, and so on. A comfortable chair by your sitting-room window can provide a life-long, absorbing hobby.

The books on pets are too numerous to mention. Have a browse in a good book shop for a couple of hours, or ask the advice of a librarian.

For direct, reliable information on most pets the following addresses will be useful.

Universities Federation for Animal Welfare, (UFAW)
8 Hamilton Close,
South Mimms,
Potters Bar,
Hertfordshire EN6 3QD.

The Kennel Club,
1 Clarges Street,
London W1Y 8AB.

The Scottish Kennel Club,
6b Forres Street,
Edinburgh EH3 6BJ.

The Feline Advisory Bureau,
350 Upper Richmond Road,
London SW15 6TL.

Pedigree Petfoods Advisory Service,
Waltham-on-the-Wolds,
Melton Mowbray,
Leicestershire LE14 4RS.

Your local veterinary surgeon.
Your local library.

3 Money: The Root of All Evil

Robert Dougall

Money certainly can, and often does, lead to evil, when treated as a commodity in its own right. On the other hand, many may feel more inclined to agree with George Bernard Shaw, who stoutly maintained that lack of money is the root of all evil.

However you plan to spend your time, you need to have a good idea of how much money you are likely to receive, whether it is income from savings, state benefits or pension.

I left school at seventeen and my first job was in a chartered accountant's office, but the work there made no sense to me, and I was only too happy to escape the loathed ledgers and files when I joined the BBC. Generally speaking, pensions seem to be one of life's great mysteries. I only know I was fortunate, in that I automatically joined the BBC's Pension Plan when I became their youngest ever radio announcer, as it happened on my twenty-first birthday.

At the risk of being repetitive: where money is concerned, planning is extremely important – and the earlier that this is done, the better.

In order to work out exactly how much money you are likely to have coming in, you need to know how much you can expect to receive from your pension, and how much in income from your savings. And, sadly, something that does not cease on retirement is the payment of income tax. Just as you probably got used to the intracies of PAYE and Schedule D, along comes a whole set of new rules, such as the Age Allowance and the Earnings Rule.

Fortunately, we have Margaret Dibben to help. As Money Editor of *The Guardian*, she is more at home than most with this particular minefield, and she will explain the ins and outs of pensions, tax and savings.

Planning and budgeting

Quite naturally, the one thing many people dread most about retirement is the anticipated drop in their standard of living. Many articles on the subject of retirement will be quick to point out that your overheads should be less, but with more leisure time on your hands, some costs may even go up. For instance, you will not have to pay for your season ticket to and from the office; on the other hand, if photography is your big passion you will probably spend more money on that. Try not to get into that silly situation where one partner secretly resents the weekly trip to the hairdressers, on the grounds of extravagance, while the other cannot understand why someone who is always going on about money then disappears off to the pub for hours at a time. Everyone needs a little self-indulgence, at any age, so discuss things in advance to work out a plan that is fair to both parties. And if you do not have anyone else to consider, it is still worth remembering that all through our lives we have very different notions about how best to use our money. Again, it is simply a question of what is best for you.

Take Joe and Maggie. They live out in the heart of the country in a beautiful little cottage. Their rates are not too high and Maggie saves quite a lot of money by growing fruit and vegetables and freezing them.

Their biggest cost is the upkeep of the car. Yet without it, instead of enjoying the peace of the countryside, they would soon begin to feel isolated. And because the bus service is so infrequent they would probably end up spending quite a lot on mini-cabs too.

For Maggie's sister Jane, it is completely different. Jane and her husband Bill live in a pleasant but modest semi in the London suburb of Hammersmith. When Bill retired last year, they decided to sell the car which he had always used for work. Parking was becoming more and more of a problem in their tiny street, and both Bill and Jane have free GLC travel passes on the buses and tubes. They much prefer spending their money on trips to the theatre or cinema and this year when they go off to Cornwall for their week's holiday they are planning to rent a car which will actually work out much cheaper overall.

Margaret Dibben.

The table on pages 40-1 will help you to spot the areas where you can expect to be better or worse off. It is just a *guide*, but it should give you some idea of how things are likely to change, and form the basis for some lively discussion.

Note: Pension rises and changes in the tax position of pensioners are announced in the April budget. Pension rises are implemented the following November. See 'Stop Press', page 96, for any relevant changes where rates are mentioned.

Your pension

Margaret Dibben

Everybody gets some sort of pension from the state but it is not very much and for some people it is a pittance. The state pension itself is divided into two sections. You may get both or you may get the basic state pension plus an occupational pension. If you had paid graduated pension contributions between 1961 and 1975, you may have a few pennies coming from this.

You might also be entitled to a supplementary pension if your income is below a very low amount.

BASIC PENSION

Exactly how much you get depends on your National Insurance contribution record. If you have paid the correct number of contributions, you will get the full basic pension whether you were an employee or self-employed. If you have not paid enough, you will get less than the full pension, small as it is.

Men can claim this at the age of sixty-five; and women when they are sixty, if they are claiming in their own right. Women reaching sixty can also claim on their husband's contributions but not until the husband is sixty-five, or later than that if he does not retire at sixty-five. But she will not get as much as if she were claiming on her own contributions.

Married women who chose to pay the reduced rate National Insurance contributions will not have any pension in their own right. But married women who pay the full amount are now entitled to credits for the time they take off work to bring up a family or to look after a severely disabled person.

ADDITIONAL PENSION

You may get a second slice on top of the basic pension. If you have been working, your employer may have decided to 'contract out' of the state scheme. If he did, then your additional pension will come in the form of an occupational pension from the company.

If your employer did not contract out, your additional pension will be an earnings-related state pension. You may be very lucky and get both an earnings-related pension because your employer did not contract out and an occupational pension as well.

If your employer had contracted out you are guaranteed a certain level of pension. This is known as the *Guaranteed Minimum Pension* or GMP. It means that you will get at least as much as you would have done if you were in the state scheme, although in practice you will quite likely get more.

The earnings-related part of the state pension scheme started in 1978 and it will not be fully operational until 1998. Anyone retiring before then will not see the full benefit.

To be eligible for an earnings-related pension, your employer must not be contracted out of the state scheme, but it does not matter what your National Insurance record is. Even if you are on a reduced basic pension, your earnings-related slice is only assessed on how much you have earned.

The figures used are earnings between, at the bottom end, the *Lower Earnings Limit*, and at the top, the *Upper Earnings Limit*. These are the two amounts which, since 1978, have determined how much, if any, National Insurance contributions you have to pay.

SUPPLEMENTARY PENSION

You can claim this if you do not have enough money to live on and you have retired. It operates similarly to supplementary benefit, meaning that you are ineligible if you have more than £3,000 in savings. (Check 'Stop Press', page 96, for 1984 rates.)

The greatest advantage is the additional help that you automatically get once you are accepted for supplementary pension. You will get free glasses, free dental treatment and help with, say, a special diet and with the cost of travelling to hospital.

You can claim supplementary pension by asking for a form SB1 at the post office. When you pick this up, also ask for a postage-paid envelope to go with it. You send this to your local social security office.

Do not be hesitant about claiming supplementary pension. It is your right and you have paid for it with income tax throughout your lifetime.

You might also be entitled to a single lump sum payment to help with large, unexpected expenses. If you have a bill you cannot meet for something essential, perhaps a piece of furniture or warm clothing, ask your DHSS office if they can help.

Even if you are not eligible for supplementary pension, you may qualify for a rent and/or rate rebate. These are now called *Housing Benefit*, and your local DHSS office can give you a leaflet on the subject or advise you further.

OVER EIGHTY

When you reach eighty, and this applies to men and women, you may be entitled to extra help that has nothing to do with your National Insurance contributions. You will automatically get a little extra pension at this age.

OCCUPATIONAL PENSION

What you get from a company pension depends on how many jobs you have had and what the terms have been. You may have one very good pension, or you may have several tiny ones from various different jobs.

You will certainly be better off if you have stayed in one job all your working life. But when you come to retire, do get in touch with all your previous employers to find out if they have any pension for you, however small. They may have tried to contact you but lost your address, or missed a change of address if you have moved.

CONTINUING WORK

You do not have to stop work at sixty-five (sixty for women) just because you have reached retirement age. If you are able to continue working, you can delay receiving the state pension, and you make no more National Insurance contributions. This is called 'cancelling' your retirement, but you can only do it once.

When you do eventually take the pension, you will get a little more than you otherwise would.

You can, if you like, continue to work but draw your pension at the same time. In this case, you must either work only occasionally, or do short hours, or earn only a little, to qualify. And you will be taxed on the money.

BUDGETING GUIDE

Income (before tax)	Before Retirement	After Retirement
Employment Part-time employment State pension Additional and/or graduated pension Private pension scheme Supplementary pension Special allowances and entitlements Investments and savings Other income (i.e., lodgers, regular gifts from children, etc.)		
Total:		
Outgoings		
Income tax National Insurance contributions Pension contributions Insurance (life/house, etc.)		
Home running expenses		

Rent or mortgage payments
Rates (general and water)
Heating and lighting bills:
  Gas
  Electricity
  Oil
  Paraffin
Telephone rental and bills
Repairs and home improvements
Servicing costs: household appliances or heating systems
General household items: loo paper, furniture polish, etc.
Garden (seeds, fertilizer, tools, etc.)
Caravan: site rent and running costs		

Food and drink		
Food at home Entertaining friends at home Food out Alcohol		

BUDGETING GUIDE

Personal spending	Before Retirement	After Retirement
Clothes		
Shoes		
Dry-cleaning/laundry/shoe repairs		
Cigarettes		
Make-up/hairdressing		
Club subscriptions		
Postage and stationery		
Newspaper/books/magazines		

Transport

	Before Retirement	After Retirement
Fares to office		
Fares general		
Car purchase loan		
Car tax		
Car insurance		
Car maintenance (servicing, etc.)		
Train fares (visiting relatives)		
Railcard		
Petrol/oil		
Motoring organization subs.		

Leisure/Hobbies/Entertainment

	Before Retirement	After Retirement
Classes		
Holidays		
Theatre/cinema		
Hobbies/sports		
Pets (vet bills/licences/food)		

Miscellaneous

	Before Retirement	After Retirement
Birthday/Christmas cards/presents		
Prescriptions		
Dentists		
Opticians		
Other		
....		
....		
....		

regarded as your working life will depend on whether you were working in a pensionable job at the time.

If you continued studying after the age of sixteen, you will be credited with National Insurance contributions.

Guaranteed Minimum Pension If your employer has contracted out of the state pension scheme, you are guaranteed to receive at least as much as you would have done if he had stayed in.

Widows' Tax Allowance This is an increased personal allowance against income tax paid in the year after the death of the husband.

Savings

Margaret Dibben

Those who have managed to accumulate a little savings before they retire will be rewarded by their thrift. But, however large a nest egg you have, you will want to make the most of your money and be sure you have it invested in the best place.

Before you decide where to put your money, there are several questions to ask yourself. These will help you understand the principles of saving.

First of all, do you pay tax? Whether or not you do, and what rate of tax you pay, makes a difference to where you should put your money. If you are a high-rate tax-payer, you should put at least some of your money into tax-free savings such as National Savings certificates.

If you pay no tax at all, you should be wary of building societies because they have to pay tax on your behalf and you cannot get it back.

Most people fall between the two extremes and pay basic rate tax. When you are comparing interest rates, always check whether the rate is before tax or after tax.

If you have a high income from savings, you may find yourself caught for the *Investment Income Surcharge*. At present, you can earn up to £7,100 a year from investments at the ordinary rate of tax. But on any money above that, you will pay an extra 15 per cent tax.

It may be that you only just have enough to pay basic rate tax on your earnings. But even so, with a high investment income, you may have to pay tax at 45 per cent.

Question number two is: how quickly will I want to get my hands on the money? If you are happy to tie your money up for long periods of time, then you can find higher rates of interest than if you are able to get it out on demand.

Thirdly, ask yourself: do I want to take a risk? If you want to know that your money is totally secure, you will get an average, or sometimes poor, return. If you are prepared to take a risk, then you might get a spectacular return; alternatively you can lose everything.

But, before you start thinking about playing the stock market, or even buying a few Granny Bonds, you should make sure you have an emergency fund that you can get at quickly for sudden unexpected bills.

Once this is taken care of, and a few hundred pounds should be enough, you can plan your investments. There are two more questions to get straight: do you have a lump sum of money to invest or do you want to put small amounts away regularly? And then, do you want to receive a regular income or can you manage without the extra income and instead see your lump sum of capital grow larger?

Here are the main saving schemes around.

NATIONAL SAVINGS

These savings schemes are run by the Government. They are totally safe and the rate of interest is always competitive and sometimes very good.

With nearly all the schemes, you have to tie your money up for long periods of time or suffer penalties if you need to get it out urgently.

National Savings Certificates

These are issued for five years and, to get the best return, you should hold on to them for the full five years. You can cash them in before then, but you will get a lower rate of interest.

The great advantage of National Savings certificates is that they are completely free of any tax.

Once a savings certificate has been issued, the rate of interest will never change. If the Government wants to alter the rate, it does so by bringing out a new certificate.

You buy them in units of £25 each and the maximum any one person can hold is £5,000, or 200 units, in the current 26th issue. But if you inherit certificates when someone dies, then you are allowed to hold more than the limit.

To buy them, you can fill in an application form at the post office or at a bank.

Index-linked National Savings Certificates

These are commonly known as Granny Bonds but now anyone, even a child, can buy them. They do not pay out a set rate of interest but your money is guaranteed to go up in line with inflation.

Whatever happens, your money keeps its purchasing power and, if you keep the certificates for five years, you get an additional 4 per cent bonus. At present Granny Bonds are also paying a 2·4 per cent annual supplement as long as you hold on to them for at least a full year.

You buy the certificates in units of £10 up to a maximum of £10,000 but if you inherit Granny Bonds you can hold more. Ask for an application form at the post office. You will not receive any money until you cash in the certificates, but you will not have to pay any tax on the money.

Monthly income bonds

These are very popular with pensioners who want to receive a little extra money each month. You must have a minimum of £2,000 to invest, and you must be prepared to put the money away and forget about it, because you lose interest if you have to get it back quickly. The maximum allowed is £200,000.

The interest you receive on monthly income bonds is taxable. If you do not have to pay tax, then you will get the full, gross, amount. You must tell the Inland Revenue about the money when you fill out your tax return.

You can ask to receive the money each month either by cheque in the post or you can have it paid direct into a bank account.

To invest, ask for a postage paid envelope from the post office, or write to the Bonds & Stock Office, Blackpool FY3 9YP. Alternatively, you can telephone Teledata on 01-200 0200 and ask for a form.

Deposit bonds

Deposit bonds will tie your money up for three months once you have held them for a full year. If you need to take your money out within the first year, you will only get half the usual rate of interest.

The only exception to this rule is when the money is paid out because the holder of the bonds has died.

You need a minimum of £500 to open a deposit bond and can only invest in multiples of £50. The maximum holding is £50,000.

Interest is paid out to you gross but tax-payers will have to tell the Inland Revenue and pay tax on the interest. For details write to the Deposit Bond Office, National Savings, Glasgow G58 1SB.

Premium bonds

These are not a good way of investing. You may have a lucky streak and win many times over the amount you put in. But on the other hand you may never win a penny. And meanwhile your money is losing value because of inflation.

Premium bonds are only for people who have enough investments elsewhere that they can afford to gamble.

National Savings Bank ordinary account

At present this account is paying a two-tier rate of interest. At best it is good for high-rate tax-payers; at worst it is poor for everybody.

If you have at least £500 to invest and you leave the money in the account for one whole calendar year, you will get the higher rate of interest. But your money must be sitting in the account on 1 January and must stay there until 31 December. Otherwise you will only get half the rate of interest. If you have less than £500 to start with you will only receive the lower rate.

The advantage to tax-payers is that the first £70 of interest you receive is completely tax free. A married couple with a joint account are allowed £140 of tax-free interest. However, if your interest goes above these figures, then you have to pay tax.

If you have an ordinary account, you can apply for a Regular Customer Account at one particular post office. This facility enables you to withdraw up to £250 a day at that one post office, although you can use your account normally anywhere else.

You can also use your National Savings Bank account to pay bills of up to £250, such as your electricity bill, TV licence, and any other bill you can settle through the post office.

You can get cash of up to £100 even if you are not a regular customer; and you can ask for regular bills to be paid by standing order from your ordinary account.

Investment account

The National Savings investment account (called Invac for short) pays a far better rate of interest than the ordinary account. But all of it is taxable.

The minimum investment is only £1 and the maximum you can put in is £200,000. You only have to give one month's notice to get your money out.

If you inherit money in an investment account, you can go over the limit. You can also keep a higher limit if you had this money in the account before July 1977.

You can either call into a post office and ask for an application form, or you can write direct to the National Savings Bank, Freepost, Glasgow G58 2BR, making a cheque payable to 'National Savings'.

BUILDING SOCIETIES

These are a very convenient place to put your money. Only in the most remote corners of the country is there no building society branch or agency. You can have your money in an ordinary share account, which pays the basic rate of interest but you have the advantage that you can get your money out by calling in and asking for it.

If you are prepared to tie your money up for longer, you can earn a better rate of interest. Each society has different schemes and you should call in at your nearest branch and ask what they can offer.

Several of them now have Monthly Income Accounts, which will pay you a regular cheque each month. This is worth asking for.

You can have an account where you put in odd amounts of money as and when you can afford it; or you can have an account which you cannot add to at all (these usually pay a guaranteed premium rate); or you can have an account where you pay in an agreed sum each month.

The big thing to remember when saving in a building society is the question of tax. The building society will pay the tax at a special rate before they pay out the interest to you. Even if you yourself are not a tax-payer, you cannot ask for the money back.

But if you are a high-rate tax-payer, you will have to pay a bit more. Even though the money comes to you tax paid, you must inform the Inland Revenue on your tax return.

Remember, when you are comparing interest rates, that most people quote the rate 'gross', while building societies quote the rate 'net', that is, after tax has been deducted.

The maximum anyone can put into one particular building society is £30,000 (or £60,000 in a joint account). But there is no limit to the number of different building society accounts you can have.

Many building societies now offer various extra bits and pieces with their accounts, such as a cheque book, a plastic card, and travellers cheques.

If you like the idea of having these extra services, look for one of these more involved accounts. But they rarely offer anything you cannot get elsewhere, so it is more important to look at the rate of interest you are offered.

BANKS

Like the building societies, the banks have a number of different schemes, including monthly income plans. The ordinary deposit account usually pays a low rate of interest and you have to pay tax on it.

Ask your local bank what they can offer and compare the interest rate with what the building societies are paying. Do not forget that the banks' rate is before tax and the building societies' is after tax.

An important question to ask is how long you will have to wait to get your money out.

If you do not like approaching one of the big four high street banks, you can have a bank account at the post office. This is the National Girobank, which operates just like any other bank account, except that you cannot run up an overdraft. You can save money in a Girobank deposit account but you must have a Girobank current account first.

The Trustee Savings bank has several deposit accounts, including one for very large sums of money (the minimum investment is £10,000). The other accounts are similar to all banks; for more information call into your nearest TSB branch and ask for details.

ANNUITIES

An annuity can provide a very good deal for pensioners, provided you live long enough. You will need to plan an annuity before your retirement; and the older you are when you start to draw the money, the better deal you will get. In any case, it is best if you are into your seventies before you start taking the money.

You can buy an annuity from an insurance company either by handing over a lump sum of money (this will need to be several thousand pounds) or by giving them smaller regular sums over a period of years.

In return, the insurance company will pay you a regular income for the rest of your life, for however long you live. But one thing you cannot do is to cancel an annuity; you cannot change your mind once you have handed over the money.

Whatever happens, once you have started an annuity, the scheme goes ahead and the insurance company will pay out for the rest of your life.

You may be able to buy an annuity by selling a part interest in your home, even though you still go on living there. For further details of such schemes see page 54.

If you want to compare deals, go to an insurance broker, tell him what you want and let him do the running around. Make sure he does a thorough job and gets several quotations for you.

GILTS

These are gilt-edged government stocks, which are totally secure. For every one you buy you are guaranteed to get £100 back when they mature but, if your timing is right, you will do much better than this.

If you want advice, ask a bank manager, a stockbroker or a financial adviser. But if you know what you are after, you can buy gilts more cheaply through the National Savings Stock Register at the post office.

STOCKS AND SHARES/UNIT TRUSTS

We have deliberately left out any advice on investing in either stocks and shares or unit trusts. Partly because the market is so speculative and you could end up losing all your money, and also because the market can change so rapidly even over a short period. If you are determined to invest your money this way do make sure you get good advice from either a reliable stockbroker or your bank manager.

Bargains, bargains . . .

If your head is reeling with figures, it is time for some *good news* on how to make your money stretch that much further. Some of the concessions and schemes mentioned here are *only* available to retired people, others apply whatever your age, but in some cases a certain amount of free time is required in order to take advantage of them.

DID YOU KNOW . . .

That many local authorities provide cheap or even *free bus* and *local train travel* to retired people. It varies from area to area, so check with your town hall to find out what is available locally.

Wherever you live a *British Rail Senior Citizen's Rail Card*, currently £12, entitles you to travel half-fare on ordinary single and return journeys and on their special offers such as Awaydays and Savers. The *Awayday* card, which is cheaper, at £7 gives you half-fares on day returns only.

For the last two years BR have had a very special offer during the month of November on these cards. In November 1983, for instance, you could travel anywhere in London and the South East (as far as Weymouth in the south and Kettering in the north) for just £2 on the full card. They will not commit themselves yet to a similar deal in 1984 but watch out for tv and press advertisements nearer the time.

Senior Citizen Rail Card holders are also entitled to buy the *Rail Europ Senior Card* for an extra £5. This entitles you to discounts ranging from 30 to 50 per cent on rail travel throughout Europe, and on Sealink ferries. Some countries in Europe will give retired people discounts without the rail card.

British Airways offer 30 per cent discounts on return domestic flights, including Jersey, provided you stay a minimum of six nights.

British Airways Reservations,
West London Air Terminal,
Cromwell Road,
London SW7.   phone: 01-370-5411

or local travel agents

Shareholders in *European Ferries* are entitled to 50 per cent discounts on regular fares on Townsend Thorensen car ferries. Minimum holding for unlimited trips is £300, but you must be a registered shareholder by February of the year in which you want to take advantage of the scheme.

European Ferries Plc,
Shareholders Concessionary Fares Department,
1 Camden Crescent,
Dover CT16 1LD.

Libraries can lend you records and tapes in addition to books. Many allow pensioners to reserve books *free*, and do not make them pay the fine. (Even so, spare a thought for the person who is waiting for it!) Use their *photocopying* facilities at 10p a time to copy out a page of useful addresses from a reference book, or recipes you want to keep. They also stock (or will get for you) a range of *large-print books* for those who have difficulty with reading.

The London Library allows you to borrow up to *ten* books at a time, for up to two months. Their Life Membership is £1,285 for, say, a twenty-five year-old, but this goes down on a sliding scale to £1,050 for those aged fifty-five and to £350 for those of seventy and over.
The London Library,
14 St James's Square,
London SW1Y 4LG.   phone: 01-930-7705

Both BBC and ITV have studio audiences for many of their programmes. Tickets are *free* if you write to the Ticket Unit, but try and give as much advance notice as possible and include a list of the type of shows you would be interested in seeing.
The BBC Ticket Unit,   (for both radio *and* tv)
Broadcasting House,
Portland Place,
London W1A 4WW.

For shows on ITV contact either your *local* Independent Television Company (address in the *TV Times*) or the makers of the particular programme you want to see: *This Is Your Life* for instance is made by Thames Television, so they would be the people to contact for tickets.

Buying *food* in bulk is *almost* always cheaper. See the section on organizing your own food co-op or bulk buying schemes on page 83.

Do not try to save money by cutting back on your insurance *cover*, but check prices of your *premiums* compared with other companies. Some offer discounts on car insurance for the over-50s and for discounts on house and contents policies for 60+ (see page 65).

NHS prescriptions are free for women over sixty and men over sixty-five. Some people also get free *glasses* and *dental* treatment. See page 43 on entitlements.

Local education classes offer a wide range of concessions depending on the area. WEA classes offer a 50 per cent reduction to pensioners, as do some of the other organizations mentioned in the section on Education, pages 19-24.

Villa-sitting in the Mediterranean can be a very cheap way of missing out on the cold British winter – think what you would save on fuel bills alone! More details of these and *Long-Stay Holidays* on pages 32-33.

Lots of concessionary schemes operate on a very local basis. Look out for signs in local shops such as shoe repairers and hairdressers.

Also check locally for discounts on *theatres* and *cinemas* (usually the afternoon performances).

Pensioners in the *south-east of England* can often enjoy a *free day trip* to *France* because the amount they save on drinks, cigarettes and local produce will more than cover the cost of the trip.

Best buys: cigarettes on the boat or hovercraft, wine (from 45p a bottle) in the local supermarket (ten bottles per person, if you can carry it!) and/or spirits (compare prices on the boat going *out* with those in the local shops and buy on the *return* journey – less carrying time). Details from your local travel agent or 'special offer' trips are sometimes advertised in the local press.

London Transport publishes a guide book listing all that is free, for all ages, in the way of amusements or entertainments in the capital. London Transport, *Free, or Almost Free, London*, 99p.

For outdoor enthusiasts, *The National Trust* reduce their Life Membership (which includes a Guest Ticket for a friend) from £300 to £200 for women of sixty and men of sixty-five. Membership entitles you to free admission to the 180 establishments open to the public in England, Wales and Northern Ireland and there is a reciprocal arrangement for The National Trust for Scotland properties.
The National Trust,
42 Queen Anne's Gate,
London SW1.　　　　phone: 01-222-9251

In Scotland, the *Scottish National Trust* Life Membership is reduced to £90 for pensioners (no guest ticket).
The National Trust for Scotland,
5 Charlotte Square,
Edinburgh E82 4DU.　phone: 031-226-5922

Provided you have already been a member of the *Royal Horticultural Society* for a period of three years before reaching retirement age, the RHS offers a five-year membership at £50 for a single person or £90 for a married couple – a saving of up to £60. This entitles you to visit the RHS Gardens at Wisley (and take in two friends free), receive two tickets for the Chelsea Flower Show, and a number of other benefits including technical advice on gardening.
The Royal Horticultural Society,
Horticultural Hall,
Vincent Square,
London SW1.　　　　phone: 01-834-4333.

For some of the concessions mentioned here,

proof of your status may be required. If your pension is paid into your bank, and you do not have a pension book, you can get an identity card from:

Central Pensions Branch,
Department of Health and Social Security,
Newcastle Upon Tyne NE98 1YX.

For a modest investment of £1.25 you can buy the English Tourist Board's excellent publication *Activity & Hobby Holidays in England*, which lists details of hundreds of interesting holidays, many of them at very reasonable prices. The Board also publishes *Let's Go*; a free guide to English hotels offering special prices for weekend breaks.

Still on the subject of money . . .
happily, one man's junk is another man's 'collector's item' . . .

As a retired bank manager, Ronald Filmer probably understands about realizing assets more than most people. But even he was staggered when he cleared out his loft last summer, found his old train set – a Basset-Locke locomotive given to him by his father in 1920 – and took it along for auction at Phillips where it sold for an amazing £850.

Phillips, Sotheby's and Christies will give you a free evaluation on all sorts of items, not just furniture and paintings. If you live out of London, or the item is too bulky to take along, send a detailed description and, if possible, a photograph or even a drawing. Always beware of people who call at the door, especially those who offer to 'take things off your hands'!
For names and addresses of reputable dealers and auctioneers write to:

British Antique Dealers Association,
20 Rutland Gate,
London SW7.

Incorporated Society of Valuers and Auctioneers,
3 Cadogan Gate,
London SW1.

4 The Englishman's Home and Castle

Robert Dougall

Once we retire, where we live becomes more important than ever. No matter how active we might plan to be, we all need a comfortable home base and the decision of whether or not to move is a vital one – and one that needs to be discussed fully by both partners.

For people who have lived all their working lives in a city, the temptation to retire to a dream house by the sea can seem a charming idea. And while it can be very satisfactory, it can also be a scenario for disaster. Roots and friends are tremendously important; without them one can wither away.

Nan and I have lived a double life for more than thirty years, but only as far as housing is concerned. We began married life in 1947 in West Hampstead, but most of our holidays we spent at the little coastal town of Southwold in Suffolk.

Five years before I retired from the BBC we sold our large rambling Victorian house in Hampstead and moved to a much smaller one, almost on the edge of the Heath. And we still try and spend as much time as possible at our cottage in Suffolk, so we feel pretty much at home in both places.

The possibilities, the options and variations available on retirement, are almost endless. Once again, there are no rights and wrongs: the important thing is to work out what suits you. One way of finding out is to make a check-list of priorities. There are some suggestions on pages 52-3, to give you a general guide, but you will have other points of your own to include.

Whether you are thinking of staying in your present home, moving to somewhere smaller nearby, or moving away completely, try putting a plus or a minus against the conditions you have at the moment (and quite rightly, probably take for granted), and against those you will encounter if you move. In this way, a picture of what is important to *you* will begin to emerge.

For instance, for some people, moving away from their children and grandchildren might be cancelled out by a healthier climate. Others might find it hard to move away from the church or chapel they have attended for years and where they have a circle of friends. For the latter the answer might be a smaller house or flat in the same neighbourhood. Remember, too, that things do not change just once, on retirement. The family doctor whose advice you rely on so much now may be retiring himself in a couple of years.

Moving

If you are serious about moving, whether buying somewhere new, making a council swap, or moving in with friends or family, do spend some time in the area, preferably in the autumn or winter, so that you see it in its everyday state. Even if this means spending a week in a hotel, it is a small investment in time and money compared to the cost of moving to somewhere that definitely doesn't suit you – and then having to move again.

Staying put . . .

OWNER/OCCUPIERS

If, having weighed up all the pro's and con's, you do decide to remain where you are, you may want to make a few changes to your house to make it easier to run, or use some of your retirement lump sum to carry out essential repairs. An important point: if there are going to be two people in the house for much of the day, it is a good idea for both of you to have a little space to yourselves. One solution could be to make the spare bedroom into a sort of hobby room. Whether your passion is making model cars or needlework, it can be very irritating to spend half a day setting everything out and then have to clear it all away just because some friends decide to drop in. If you do not have a spare room, what about building an extension for this purpose? While you are thinking about work on the home, check areas such as wiring, the woodwork and the roof.

If you decide to take out a loan from the bank or building society for work on the home, some of the interest on that loan may be tax deductible. It depends on whether or not such work will add to the capital value of the property. For instance, if you simply repair a leaking roof, this does *not* qualify for tax relief. On the other hand, if you were to put in an attic extension (which would include any work needed to be done on the roof) this would qualify for tax relief on the interest on the loan (for further information, see the section on tax relief, page 43).

If you do want to make improvements to your home, but don't want to touch your savings or take out a further loan, there are two other sources of help at hand:

Home improvement grants

Mortgage annuity or home reversion scheme

HOME IMPROVEMENT GRANTS

These are administered by the local authority and fall into three main types:

Intermediate Grant

This grant can help cover the cost of basic amenities, such as a fixed bath or shower, if you do not have one, or an indoor WC, or running hot water. You may have to wait some time while your application is being processed. But you can use the grant to cover one basic amenity, and reapply for a further grant to cover another amenity, if you need to do so. To qualify for this grant, your home must have been built or converted before 1961. If your home lacks a basic amenity, you have a *right* to this grant.

Repairs Grant

If your home needs major and structural repairs, and it was built before 1919, you can apply for a repairs grant. Unlike intermediate grants, repair grants are discretionary, and vary from one local authority to the next.

Improvement Grant

This is intended for the improvement of homes to a good standard. It should cover major alterations, such as modernizing your kitchen. Improvement grants are usually more difficult to obtain than intermediate grants or repair grants.

To qualify for any of these grants, the rateable value of your home must not be more than £225 (£400 in the Greater London area). The grants generally cover 75 per cent of the cost of improvements or repairs and you provide the remaining 25 per cent.

It is a slow business applying for a renovation grant. It can take many months and as with anything that involves local government bureaucracy, a lot of patience. If you begin repairs or improvements before the local authority grant is approved, you will forfeit your chance of getting one.

To find out more about any of these grants, the procedure is to go through your local council housing department (the home improvement section), or to the council's environmental health department.

In addition to the home improvement *grants* given by local authorities, there are also local authority *loans*. If you get a maturity loan from the council's financial department you have to pay back the interest for an agreed period only, or until the house is sold or becomes part of your estate. The local authority then takes back the capital part of the loan.

If the local authority decides to give you this type of loan, it will hold the title deeds to the property as security. But you still own your own home.

Help the Aged Housing Trust and Anchor Housing Trust both publish useful booklets on the various types of help available to older owner/occupiers.

For most of us, our home is probably our most valuable possession, and if you bought your house or flat many years ago, today it is probably worth several times the price you paid.

While it is nice to think you have something to pass on to your children or relatives, chances are

Social and emotional considerations	Staying Put	Moving Nearby	Moving Away
Pleasant neighbourhood			
Peace and quiet of the country			
Stimulus of a town or city			
Feeling of isolation			
Present circle of close friends			
Will I make new friends quickly			
Children (near/far away)			
Grandchildren (near/far away)			
Other family (near/far away)			
Links with church/chapel/synagogue			
Local activities: politics or clubs			
Healthier climate			
Opportunities for part-time or voluntary work			
High level of health care locally			

Practical and financial considerations

	Staying Put	Moving Nearby	Moving Away
Public transport free			
(buses) subsidized			
no concessions			
frequent/infrequent			
Trains			
Car a necessity (both partners able to drive?)			
Good local shops			
Post office			
Good local library			
Local education classes			
wide choice			
free/subsidized/no concessions			
Local entertainment			
Cinemas or theatres			

Gains/losses and options

	Staying Put	Moving Nearby	Moving Away
Cheaper accommodation + lump sum			
Conversion of present property			
Room to take in lodgers or students			
Rates (cheaper/more expensive)			
Annuity or home income plan possible			
Small flat in town + home or caravan in the country			

The home itself	Staying Put	Moving Nearby	Moving Away
Cost of moving: solicitors' fees, surveys, etc.			
Space for friends and family to stay			
Heating/insulation (more or less expensive)			
Sufficient storage space			
Smaller/larger garden/no garden at all			
Room for a pet			
Space to pursue a hobby			
Easier to run			
Any outlay for new carpets/curtains/wardrobes, etc.			
Flat			
House			

you have thought from time to time about what good use you could put the money to now. If you are in your late sixties or seventies you *can* use some of that money now – and still live in the same house. There are no rules about what you do with the extra cash either. It can provide a regular weekly income, to add to your present pension; you can spend it on a once in a lifetime holiday, if you like, or use it to do the improvements discussed earlier. Sounds too good to be true . . . There are two main types of scheme:

MORTGAGE ANNUITY SCHEME
(sometimes called a Home Income Plan)
Assuming that your home has increased in value since you bought it, you arrange a mortage through an insurance company. This will give you a lump sum. This lump sum is invested to buy an annuity which provides you with an income. The capital used to buy the annuity is paid back when the house is eventually sold. Until then, you continue to own your home. Different companies have different rules about age qualifications for this scheme, but it is usually seventy or over, or, in the case of married couples, a combined age of 150.

Life Offices Association,
Aldermay House,
Queen Street,
London EC4P 4JD.   phone: 01-248-4477

They will send you a full list of companies operating home income schemes.

The Abbey National Building Society,
Head Office,
27 Baker Street,
London W1M 2AA.   phone: 01-486-5555

The Building Trust,
Stationers Hall Court,
30-32 Ludgate Hill,
London EC4M 7ND.   phone: 01-236-0860
Offers special home income schemes for 60+, as well as mortgages for first-time buyers.

Hambro's Provident Assurance Ltd,
25 Green Street,
London W1Y 4HQ.   phone: 01-499-0631

Help the Aged,
The Court House,
Ward Street,
Guildford,
Surrey.   phone: Guildford (0483) 571772
Operate *The Gifted Housing Scheme* for converting large old properties into flats, providing original owner with free flat.

Under the above schemes you have really acquired a further mortgage on your property. Another scheme to provide you with extra income works rather differently – and requires some hard thinking, and expert advice. This is the . . .

53

HOME REVERSION SCHEME

Under this scheme, you *sell* your interest in your home – or at least a part of it – to a financial institution, in order to buy an annuity and/or a lump sum. But you still live in your home, and you are still responsible for maintenance and repairs. The companies who operate reversion schemes are:

Home Reversions Ltd,
30 Windsor Place,
Cardiff.   phone: Cardiff (0222) 371726

Inishowen Ltd,
253 High Street,
Aldershot,
Hampshire.   phone: Aldershot (0252) 311531

Investment Properties Reversions Ltd,
108 Stafford Road,
Wallington,
Surrey.   phone: 01-669-9444

Residential Home Reversions Ltd,
83 Grand Avenue,
Worthing,
West Sussex BN11 58D.   phone: Worthing
(0903) 49903

PRIVATE RENTED ACCOMMODATION

If you are a private tenant, and you do not wish to move home in retirement, it is important to know that your landlord is normally responsible for maintaining the building and amenities such as water, gas and electricity. However, if your tenancy dates from before 1961, you may be responsible for some repairs. So it is useful to check with your Citizens' Advice Bureau, law centre or housing aid centre, before trying to get your landlord to carry out repairs.

As for improvements and the provision of basic amenities, you can suggest to your landlord that he apply to the council for a renovation grant, if there is a need for major work. Where repairs are needed, it is best to let your landlord or his agent know in writing, rather than by telephone, and keep copies of all correspondence. And if the defects could be considered a danger to your health or safety – for instance, dry rot, or dangerous electrical wiring – then the environmental health officer from the local council can insist that the landlord carries out the repairs. If there is no danger, but the landlord refuses to carry out the repairs you wish, you can ask for legal advice from a law centre, a Citizens' Advice Bureau or a housing aid centre.

COUNCIL RENTED ACCOMMODATION

If you are already a council tenant there are a number of special schemes to help if you are interested in moving home. The Housing Department of your local council will be able to tell you more about them.

Two of the most interesting are:

The National Mobility Scheme

Under this scheme, most local councils keep aside a few of their available homes to 're-let' to people from outside who want to move into the area for 'social reasons' – and that includes the need to be near relatives in old age.

The Tenants Exchange

This exchange – mainly for council or housing association tenants – allows you to swop with another tenant in a different area.

Another option for council tenants wanting to move is to put an advertisement in either *Exchange and Mart* or in the local paper in the area you want to move to.

Some councils have property specially for retired people in other areas. The Greater London Council, for instance, has a number of specially built bungalows and flats in places like Clacton and Weston-Super-Mare. Needless to say, they are very popular and so waiting lists can be long, but check to find out what is available in your area.

Some councils have now started building smaller flats specially for retired people on ordinary housing estates. So you may find it is possible to give up your larger family home and move to somewhere that is easier to run, and cheaper to heat, but where you will still be near your friends and family. The Housing Department will be pleased to give you further information because if you move into something smaller this releases accommodation for a larger family.

See also the section on 'Sheltered Accommodation', pages 55-6.

Whether you are living in council or private accommodation you may well be eligible for some financial help with your rent and/or rates. The old rent and rate rebates have now been amalgamated into a new rather complicated scheme called 'Housing Benefit', check on page 39 to find out what you are entitled to, or if you find it confusing check with the local branch of the DHSS.

If you do decide to move house in retirement, you may choose to buy a new home privately. But there are other options you might wish to consider before arriving at a decision.

Becoming a council or housing association tenant

If you want to become a council tenant, ask the Housing Department at your local authority for an application form. You may be put on the waiting list for accommodation, although some councils could have special residency requirements. And their waiting lists may not be open to people who presently own their homes. Housing associations build or renovate accommodation, usually for rental. Their purpose is to meet the needs of the community, so housing associations are supported by the Government through the Housing Corporation. Many of their homes are newly built, and some are specially designed for older people.

Find out which housing associations have property in your area. You can ask your local housing department, or a housing aid/advice centre. The next stage would be to write to the associations you find attractive, and request an application form.

Councils and housing associations are responsible for major repairs to their accommodation. Council tenants can telephone the environmental health officer; he will inspect the property, and decide whether defects like faulty wiring or a blocked lavatory are serious enough for urgent repair. If you have a problem with your house or flat, and really do not seem to be getting anywhere with the council, get in touch with one of your two *ward councillors*. You can find out their names from the town hall. It is their responsibility to help you sort your problem out.

It is also worth knowing that all council tenants and some housing association tenants can now buy their own homes, provided they have lived in them for more than three years. If you are a sitting tenant, you may be able to pay only 60 per cent of market value of the property, depending on the length of your tenancy.

Before you buy, do consider that, as the owner, you will be responsible for all maintenance, repairs and insurance. If, nonetheless, you would like to go ahead, you can get a Right To Buy Claim Form from your local housing department, or, if you are a housing association tenant, from the association office. For further information, the Department of the Environment publish a leaflet, *Right to Buy*, available at housing aid centres and Citizens' Advice Bureaux.

Special housing for older people

Housing associations and many councils have built self-contained flats or bungalows specially designed for older people. These offer residents the advantage of living in a community, with the services of a warden on call. This type of housing is called sheltered, or wardened, accommodation. Some housing associations, like Anchor and Hanover, specialize in this type of sheltered accommodation. In these homes, there is often an alarm system and a warden, in case of emergency.

If you are considering this type of accommodation, it is useful to look out for factors such as convenient layout and design. Rented sheltered housing is provided only by councils and housing associations; in all such housing, a warden is in attendance, but he is not always resident in some sheltered accommodation. There are usually about thirty homes on a site. On most sites, social activities are organized for those who want them, but it should still be possible for you to be alone when and if you want.

Lotte Glover was a bit surprised when Solihull Council offered her 'sheltered' accommodation in a tower block. She was already familiar with the estate and had heard the tales of vandalism, broken lifts and a host of other problems. But when she went to look she was amazed at the changes made as part of the Council's refurbishment scheme. Entryphones and a warden meant that security was no longer a problem. And without noisy teenagers riding up and down all day, the two lifts were perfectly adequate. The reception area now had fitted carpet, and a series of pot plants gave it a welcoming appearance. Best of all, Lotte discovered, there was a separate 'common room' where residents could drop in for a game of bingo or a friendly chat – without having to walk back home afterwards on a dark night in the freezing cold.

Lotte's been living in Woodbrooke House for some time now and says she would not swop it for anything. Her unexpected bonus? The constantly changing view from her window from which she can see for miles around.

Normally, if you live in sheltered accommodation, you will not be able to buy your home. However, there are some housing associations, and a few private developers, which allow you to buy sheltered housing. Most of these schemes offer more or less the same facilities as council sheltered accommodation, although often in more luxurious surroundings. You pay a lump sum for a long lease, on the understanding that you can either sell it back to the developer for a fixed amount, or alternatively it becomes part of your estate on your death. In addition to the cost of the lease, you will also need to set aside a certain amount of money to cover the service charges for the facilities provided.

The standard and costs of these schemes vary greatly, so if you are interested make sure you visit several and talk to people who have lived there for some time. Find out as much as you can about the standard of the services provided, and work out an estimate of their running costs.

Sheltered accommodation is really designed for people who are perhaps too frail to live on their own but who are still basically fit. If you become seriously incapacitated, it may be necessary to exchange your sheltered accommodation for somewhere that has more nursing facilities available. For further information, contact the Housing Department at your local council, or a local Housing Aid Centre or Housing Advice Centre (ask the town hall for the number).

RESIDENTIAL HOMES

There may come a time when even special sheltered accommodation is not enough to help you cope with everyday living, especially if you are feeling lonely, or your health is poor. It is helpful to have a chat with your doctor, or a social worker, a friend or relative. There may be community and social services available in your area to provide you with a home help, Meals on Wheels, a day centre and so on. But if you feel you would prefer to live in a home run by the local authority, you can apply to their social services department. They will assess your need. If you visit a home and you do not like it, you may refuse it, and wait for an offer in another home. The fees for these local authority homes vary according to your needs. The minimum charge is currently £27.25 a week.

Voluntary homes are non-profit making, and are run by registered charities. During your working life you may have joined a professional body or trade union. Many of these provide residential homes for their retired members so it is worth writing to them to see if they have any vacancies.

There are also a number of private residential homes. The charge for these is usually between £80 and £100 per week, sometimes more, but your local social services department can 'sponsor' people in private or voluntary homes, if the department feels that the need is urgent. And if you qualify for supplementary benefit, the DHSS can help by paying you a local 'residential care' rate of benefit, as well as other allowances to help meet the cost of the home.

Moving Home in Retirement, 85p, SHAC, 189a Old Brompton Road, London SW5.

The Anchor Guide To Staying Put In Retirement, £2.50, The Anchor Trust, 10 St Cross Road, Oxford OX1 3TU.

Your Housing In Retirement, Age Concern England, 60 Pitcairn Road, Mitcham, Surrey.

Living abroad

Finally, retirement may be just the right time to start thinking about castles in Spain: living in them, not just dreaming about them.

If you are thinking of buying property abroad to retire to, there are a number of very important points to consider. If you have regularly visited the same place for holidays, you may already have a small network of friends there, which is obviously a big plus. On the other hand you would be well advised to spend more time in that area *out of season* to find out what it is really like.

One way to do this, without actually committing yourself, is to 'villa-sit' for a few months. There are a number of companies that are always looking for guardians for villas or apartments in the Mediterranean. You pay a nominal weekly charge and the operating companies can often offer flights at very cheap rates. Or you could try home-swopping: exchanging your house or flat with a family living in the area you are considering, just for a month or so, to see how you get on. A third option is to go on a 'long-stay' holiday. Several companies organize these, usually in the off-peak season, at very reasonable rates.

Any of these would give you a chance to get the feel of the place; to decide whether cheap wine makes up for paying three times as much for your daily paper, or watching television in a language you do not really understand. (Details of villa-sitting, home-swops and long-stay holidays are given on pages 32-3.)

PENSION RIGHTS

Your basic state pension can be paid to you, free of UK tax in any country in the world. Some countries have reciprocal arrangements with the UK, so any pension increases given by the Government here are added to your pension each year. Other countries have no such agreement, so

the state pension you are receiving now would be 'frozen', and you will receive the same in twenty years time as you do now. The choice is arbitrary too: if you go to Jamaica, you will get the increases. If you go to the Leeward Islands you will not. If you go to Spain (or any of the EEC countries) you will get the pension rises, if you go to Australia or Canada, you will not.

For a full list of the countries who do have reciprocal agreements, contact the DHSS.

HEALTH CARE

The cost and standard of health care abroad is extremely variable. Spain, for instance, actually has a better record than the UK when it comes to treating kidney disease in older people. But if you take off for a remote Greek island, it would obviously be unrealistic to expect anything like the level of care available here. The main points to check in the area you are proposing to move to are: do they have an agreement with the UK for reciprocal health care; does your present private insurance (if you have one) cover medical costs abroad? Are the facilities available in that particular area sufficient for your needs (both now and in the years to come)? Is there some form of local medical insurance you can take out and how much will it cost/what does it cover? The DHSS may be able to give you some guidance, but if there is already a retired British 'colony' it obviously makes sense to ask them.

Furnell, M., *Buying Overseas Property*, *General Guide*

First aid for the house

In Chapter 1 we mentioned the importance of each partner letting the other into some of his or her 'secrets'. Sadly, if the *Years Ahead* postbag is anything to go by, far too many people do not do this until it is too late. For a woman who has just lost her husband, the sheer frustration of not being able to change a fuse is the last straw. Which is why we were unashamedly sexist in choosing a very capable woman, Zena Skinner, for our do-it-yourself spot on the programme.

Zena Skinner.

Here is her top ten of things you should be able to fix around your house.

Zena Skinner

When things go wrong in the home, and you have not been used to coping with them, the first feeling is one of panic, so the following should help you to cope:

1. Make sure you know where the electricity and gas meters are, how to read them, and how to turn the supply off from the mains.

    Make sure you know how to operate the central heating system. Most work with a time clock so that you can either have round-the-clock heating, or have the system turning itself on and off when you want. Learn how to 'bleed' the radiators. This means letting out the air which accumulates over a period of time but which prevents the hot water circulating effectively.

    Leaking water can cause serious problems, so find out where to turn the main water supply off inside and/or outside the house.

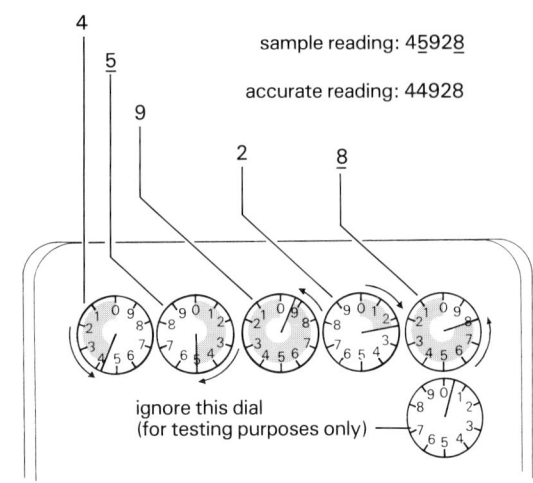

When you are reading your meter, gas or electric, always read the dials from left to right, and also keep in mind adjacent dials revolve in opposite directions.

How to read an electric meter: *Write down the number the pointer has passed on each dial. If the pointer is directly over a number, write that number down but underline it. We now have a sample reading of 45928. Look at the underlined numbers again. Is one of these followed by a 9? If so, reduce the underlined number by 1, which will give us an accurate reading of 44928.*

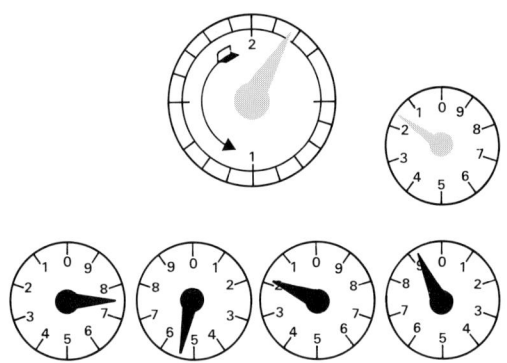

How to read a gas meter: *Only read the numbers on the bottom four dials. Where the pointer is between two numbers, write down the lower one. However, if the pointer is between 9 and 0 you should put down 9. The reading for this meter is 7519.*

To find out how many units of gas or electricity you have used, simply subtract the number from the previous reading (shown on your last bill) from your new reading.

2. Wiring a plugtop is simple if you do it step by step.

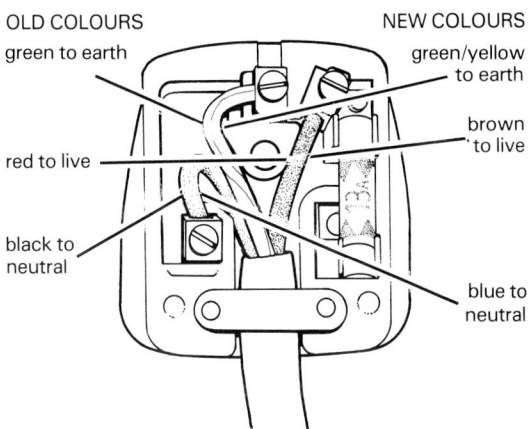

OLD COLOURS
green to earth
red to live
black to neutral

NEW COLOURS
green/yellow to earth
brown to live
blue to neutral

Do check the colour of the flexes when changing a plug as the colour code was changed a few years ago.

The Electrical Association for Women have produced a tea-towel which also illustrates this, and they run courses on electricity for housewives.
Electrical Association for Women,
25 Foubert's Place,
London W1V 2AL.

3. It is essential that the correct fuse is fitted to the plug of each appliance, so check with this chart:

3 amp fuse	for most appliances up to 700 watts (this information will be given on the plate at the back or base of the appliance)
5 amp	lighting circuit
13 amp	appliances rated over 700 watts e.g., fridge
15/20 amp	immersion heater
30 amp	ring main circuit and the average cooker
45 amp	large cooker

4. It is very frustrating to have to hunt for the fuse wire *after* the lights have gone out, so always have an emergency kit by the electricity meter. This should include: fuse wire, cartridge fuses, screwdriver, pliers, and torch.

A candle and matches are also useful, but, for safety's sake, you should put the candle in an old cup or mug. It is much easier to carry a lit candle around in this way – rather than on a saucer.

5. If the sink gets blocked up and you have an outside drain: block up the pipe that is just above the drain, then dissolve a handful of washing soda in boiling water. Pour this down the sink and leave for about half an hour; then unplug the pipe outside and it should be cleared. If not, you could try a suction sink-unblocker (available from hardware shops) or you could try using a plastic-covered curtain wire. Push it down the plug-hole, and then move it up and down several times. If it still has not cleared, you may feel brave enough to tackle removing the U bend first placing a large bowl underneath it. If you do not want to do this yourself, you will have to call a plumber, but watch how he fixes it – then you will know next time.

A plunger can be used to clear a blocked sink. Stop up the overflow with a wet cloth to block off the air, fill the bottom of the sink with water and place the plunger over the plug-hole. Pump the plunger up and down as hard as you can. Hopefully, the pressure of air created by this action will clear the blockage in the waste-pipe and the water will begin to drain away.

9. The term 'hypothermia' means a low body temperature and it is generally accepted that below 95°F or 35°C, hypothermia can be said to exist. People are more at risk in the winter months and one of the main dangers is that the sufferer does not feel cold. As the body temperature drops, so does the pulse rate. This can result in drowsiness and, eventually, death.

   To prevent this, have regular hot meals and drinks. Keep as active as possible, even when you are in bed. Regularly exercise your hands and feet. If you have any doubt regarding the safe temperature of the rooms in which you live, buy a thermometer and check it regularly.

10. When we have particularly hard winters, most of us have a frozen pipe somewhere in the house, usually the one on an outside wall. What I do to try and unfreeze it, is to use a hand-held hairdrier with the switch at *cold* and move this along the surface of the pipe. Putting a hairdrier on cold will sometimes work because the cold air from the drier is warmer than the ice in the pipe. But *do not* try and speed things up by putting the hairdrier on hot – you will only succeed in cracking the pipe.

For more details about safety and accidents in the home, get a copy of the ROSPA/Age Concern leaflet No. HS 175, *Home Safety: Care of Elderly People*.

The Gas and Electricity Boards have a number of useful leaflets on making the most of their services – available at showrooms.

Gardening

What sort of gardener are you? One of those whose idea of gardening is reading a book about it in a deck-chair in the sun? Or the sort who gets real pleasure from standing back to admire the row of bedding plants you have just put in?

Whichever you are, now could be a good time to think about some reorganization in the garden. Low-maintenance gardening seems to be the phrase of the moment, but what exactly does it mean?

At its best, the low-maintenance garden will have all the colour, fragrance and visual splendour of the traditional garden – with a lot less work. For instance:
– replacing a muddy, balding lawn with paving, bricks or gravel will make it less of a death trap in winter and you will have a warm, dry, maintenance-free patio in the summer.
– add to this tubs or containers of flowers and shrubs, which will need watering but should remain weed and slug-free. (You can make tubs very cheaply from large, barrel-shaped polythene containers, cut in half and given a coat of white paint.)

However much you love gardening, no one enjoys back-ache, so raised beds make planting (and weeding) less of a chore.

Many tools and gadgets have appeared on the market recently, such as the one illustrated below, that take the strain out of gardening jobs.

Raised beds make planting and weeding much easier.

A small, lightweight barrow which is an ideal aid for tidying up the garden.

The replacement of large areas normally given over to summer bedding with shrubs and perennials can give you a variety of colour and interesting foliage to last throughout the year.

Necessity, they say, is the mother of invention, and this certainly applies to the most imaginative labour-saving tools that have appeared on the market in the last few years, because many of them have been designed with disabled people in mind. There is a whole range of tools on the market now that save hours of unnecessary work, and you need not be disabled to take advantage of them. But if you have had an illness of some kind, a stroke perhaps, some of the tools now available mean that you can still enjoy your favourite hobby.

Rose, Graham, *The Low Maintenance Garden* (Windward, 1983), £7.95.
White, Andrew, *Equipment for the Disabled: Leisure and Gardening*, £3.30, + 80p p&p.
This book is available from Nuffield Orthopaedic Centre, Headington, Oxford OX3 7LD (cheques payable to Oxford AHA).
Cloet, A. and Underhill, C., *Gardening Is For Everyone* (Souvenir Press, 1982), £4.95.

Security that makes sense

It is a sad fact of life that many older people live in great fear of being attacked, either inside or outside their homes. Whilst recent crime statistics showed that older people are *less* likely to be attacked than younger (and, theoretically, richer) people, the stories that hit the headlines do not help to alleviate the fears many people have. To put things in perspective, believe it or not, the odds of being injured or 'mugged' are about the same as those of a major win on the Premium Bonds!

But on a practical level, what can be done to help? Where should you start?

You should begin with your own *Crime Prevention Officer*. Your local police station will arrange for an officer to call on you. He can tell you at a glance which are the most vulnerable areas in *your* home, and advise you on the best safety measures to take. He may well suggest:

– a spy hole in the front door that enables you to see your visitor *before* you let him or her in;
– a chain on the front door that enables your caller to hand over his identification for you to check *before* opening the door fully;
– good locks on doors and windows.

Many burglars are young amateurs, so if your house looks well protected, quite often they will not bother. It is just too much trouble, better to try up the road where they have thoughtfully left a key under the mat.

If you spend all your time worrying about the possibility of being attacked or burgled your life will become unbearable, but there are certain basic precautions which *are* sensible:

– if someone claims they are from the gas board or housing department, and if you are on your own, ask them to come back a little later when you can arrange to have a neighbour there with you. If they are *bona fide* they will not mind.
– And *never* hand over money to someone you do not know who arrives unexpectedly on your doorstep.

Sometimes the con-man's tale is very plausible – he would not make a living at it otherwise. Not long ago, one lady received a visit from a respectable looking chap who said he was from the CID, investigating forged notes in the area. He asked her to get whatever cash she had in the house and having 'inspected' her notes for some time announced he would have to take them down to the station for further examination. She never saw him, or her money, again.

If being attacked in the street is something you worry about, you could buy a 'screech alarm'. This tiny device, about the size of a small perfume spray, lets off the most appalling screeching noise when you press a button or pull the top off (you can wear it on a cord round your neck). If it makes you *feel* safer, it is worth it for that alone, and they only cost about £1 from chemists or hardware stores.

If you should be so unlucky as to be the victim of a theft or an attack, remember you are not on your own. The Victim Support Scheme may well have a branch in your area and they will offer practical help as well as a sympathetic ear.

National Association of Victim Support
Schemes,
34 Electric Lane,
London SW9 8JT.   phone: 01-737-2010/9

Do make sure too that your insurance is up to date and the cover sufficient. One company that offers special rates to people of sixty and over (and does not insist on a minimum amount of cover) is:

North London Reliance (Insurances) Ltd,
158 High Road,
East Finchley,
London N2.   phone: 01-883-1189

Age Concern run a special lower cover insurance scheme for older people. For details, contact your local branch.

Wills and funerals

Wills and funerals are things that many of us do not care to contemplate in advance. The very idea seems to underline our own mortality. But please remember, careful planning can make an enormous difference financially, and relieve a lot of suffering for partners, family and friends, particularly at a time when they are least able to cope.

There are a number of things that can be done now to minimize the problems later.

Firstly, the question of wills. Have you already made one? And if you have, do you know if recent legislation has affected your original plans? If you have not made a will at all, see your solicitor and instruct him about what you would like to go to whom from your estate. Include any specific bequests, and mention to him any special arrangements regarding where you would like to be buried or cremated, or special music you would like to have at your funeral. You will also need to appoint one or more executors – up to four in fact – although two is the usual number. You can appoint your solicitor as your executor, but he will charge extra for this, so either your children or other relatives would probably be a better idea.

You can, of course, buy a blank form from a stationers and make out your own will, but unless the instructions are *very simple* indeed it is better to get professional advice. They say solicitors make far more money sorting out the tangles resulting from home-made wills than they do from drawing up new ones!

SUPPOSING I DO NOT MAKE A WILL?

You will die 'intestate', which although not quite as nasty as it sounds, means your estate will be governed by the rules of intestacy. These rules decide who shall inherit what, and in certain cases there may be restrictions on the way in which money can be invested. It will not cover any special requests you might have considered, and it could mean paying away more of your estate in taxes.

If you have already made a will, perhaps some years ago, it would be worth having another look at it to see if it needs revising. Changes in the law, particularly tax law, can alter the original intention of a will quite dramatically. Your accountant, bank manager or solicitor will be pleased to advise you.

You can deposit your will *free of charge* with either your solicitor or your bank manager.

One final thing the family *will* thank you for is an up-to-date list of your documents and other relevant information. *Age Concern* have produced an excellent form to help you with this. It has space for you to list insurance policy numbers, and the whereabouts of the policy, building society savings, and shares, as well as things like your tax office, and national insurance number. There is even space for you to list people you would like to be informed – your old school or regiment, for instance. It has four well set out pages enabling you to list every piece of information your family could possibly need, and could well save them hours of sad work looking through old papers for information. Available from *Age Concern*, price 25p.

FUNERALS: THE FINANCIAL ASPECT

Even the simplest funeral is likely to cost around £400 – yet the death grant still stands at £30. Obviously further provision is necessary, and there are various options.

You could put aside an appropriate sum to

cover funeral costs – topping it up to keep pace with inflation. The main problem is that this capital, added to even a small amount of savings, may make you ineligible for various state benefits to which you would otherwise be entitled.

Another possibility is to take out a small life insurance policy for, say, around £1,000, specifically to cover funeral costs. Starting a new scheme in later life can be quite costly, but the premiums will be around £6 a month for a man aged seventy and slightly less for a woman.

Some funeral directors are willing to accept money for a pre-paid funeral, but the drawback here is that the company might go into liquidation before you die; or you may move away from the area, rendering the services of that particular company impractical.

The best source to advise you on all these matters is the National Association of Funeral Directors. Make sure that any firm you choose is a member. They have drawn up a Code of Practice, after consultations with the Office of Fair Trading, and they also have a complaints procedure for those who do not feel they have received good service. As with any other major outlay, it does pay to shop around. However, because few people have the opportunity to do so at the time of bereavement, it is a good idea to ask friends who have recently faced this situation for their recommendations.

Finally, do make sure you read the small print very carefully on any forms that you sign. Some companies give a discount for prompt payment. Others actually *add* a penalty payment of up to 2½ per cent *per month* while the bill remains unpaid. If you do not notice it, and the company does not remind you, this soon adds up. In their defence, funeral directors claim they would otherwise lose money. And they say they always explain their terms in great detail before going ahead. But for anyone who has just suffered a death in the family, it is the worst time to try and concentrate on anything or absorb even the simplest information, which is another good reason for getting as many things sorted out in advance as possible.

5 An Apple a Day

Robert Dougall

As in all other aspects of retirement, health problems vary tremendously according to the individual – and in many cases worrying about health can sometimes be as much of a problem as illness itself. To begin with, it is important to differentiate between the natural signs of ageing – like wrinkles and grey hair – and those that should serve as a warning that something is wrong, a persistent cough, for example, or pains in the chest.

If you are worried, see your own GP and do not be fobbed off. You have probably heard by now the tale of the ninety-year-old who went to the doctor with a painful left knee. His doctor was one of the 'you have to expect it at your age' school, but as his patient pointed out, 'the right knee is the same age, and there's nothing wrong with that'.

It is obviously a very bad idea to change the habits of a lifetime overnight. On the other hand, heavy smoking and excessive drinking are two habits we would all feel better for kicking – quite apart from the immense boost to our finances. However, if we all became strong-minded overnight the Chancellor of the Exchequer would be biting his nails to the quick – so moderation is the answer to all things.

Of course, it is much easier to give advice than to take it, and in my case, having been a confirmed smoker from the tender age of fourteen, it took three bouts of pneumonia – for which I had to be admitted to hospital, the last at the age of fifty – to convince me to give up.

Even then, I was fortunate in that I was recuperating in our Suffolk cottage on my own – away from the temptation of other people who smoked. I also stocked up with some good Burgundy, and sucked ferociously strong peppermints. But the plan seemed to work, because I

have not had even one cigarette or cigar since then and I consider it perhaps my greatest achievement, as I am not noted for my strength of will – quite the reverse in fact.

But for those who do make the effort, the rewards can be tremendous. It is not just physical well-being but also mental health that is affected. The notion that a healthy mind goes with a healthy body is back in favour again, and not before time. If you are leading an active life you will hardly have time to notice the occasional twinge here or there. But if you slump in the armchair all day, there is not much else to dwell on but where the next ache or pain is coming from.

The recent cuts in the NHS have naturally given rise to alarm, particularly amongst older people. But let us also remember that modern medicine is very sophisticated and can cure, or at least alleviate, illnesses that in the past would have meant certain, and often painful, death, even in our parents' day. Help is on hand in many forms: hearing aids, glasses and so on, and as Health Minister, Kenneth Clark, pointed out some time ago, people are now complaining about long waiting lists for operations, such as hip replacements, that simply would not have been possible even ten years ago.

So, the best advice is be sensible. After my own great achievement – giving up smoking – I was lying in the bath one day when I noticed a rounded protuberance almost obscuring my feet. I was indubitably developing a corporation. The scales confirmed that I had put on 16 lb in six weeks. My physician's advice was short and to the point: 'Knock off bread and potatoes and you'll soon be back to normal.' And of course he was right.

So, stay as active as possible (and the next few pages are full of suggestions as to how), and then try to *forget about your health* as far as you are able to.

It is unfortunate, perhaps, that every family seems to boast one relative who smoked three packets of cigarettes and drank a bottle of whisky a day and still lived to be a hundred and two. But why find out the hard way that you are *not* going to be that rare exception that proves the rule?

Exercise

Penny Copple, SRN, is Director of Development and Training at EXTEND, a registered charity which specializes in Exercise Training for the Elderly and/or Disabled. EXTEND run classes for retired people of all ages – their oldest student is an amazing ninety-nine. Penny is naturally a staunch believer in keeping fit, and here she gives her reasons – including a few you may not have thought of.

Penny Copple

Fitness fanatics, joyful joggers: the terms alone are enough to make some of us slump even further into the retirement armchair.

It is easy to convince ourselves that we are too old to start, and we shy away from the fitness fever that is currently sweeping the country.

Yet, each person in retirement has a personal responsibility to himself or herself to get the most out of life. Whether or not we wish to believe it, 'Movement is Life', and 'Stagnation is Death'.

You have only to look at the sea to take in the picture of life – the ebb and flow of the tide, movement never ceasing. Stagnation is the opposite – the green, slime-covered pond whose stream became sludgy and then blocked, circulation ceasing, life submerged. In the same way, your body can be full of movement and life, or it can be submerged through inactivity into lifelessness, listlessness and stagnation. So what can be done to stop the rot setting in.

Members of the Women's League of Health and Beauty enjoy a session in Hyde Park.

side of the square is equally strong and working harmoniously, one part with another.

physical   mental

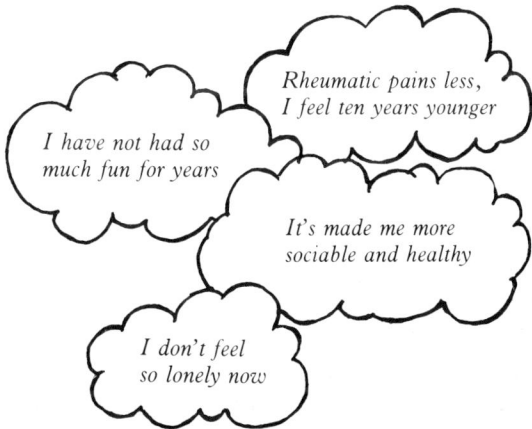

emotional   spiritual

A good example is the way we feel after we have had a brisk walk in the fresh air – warmer, brighter, fresher; and the bothersome problems diminish.

Rheumatic pains less, I feel ten years younger

I have not had so much fun for years

It's made me more sociable and healthy

I don't feel so lonely now

Betty Brandon, who suffers from arthritis, nevertheless continues to teach tap-dancing classes.

The answer is, that your body has an almost magical property – its muscles are elastic and, unlike the elastic used to keep up your clothes, which finally does lose its spring, the muscles of your body *can* be revitalized through gentle movement.

'Surely I'm too old to start exercising – it is dangerous at my age.'

You do not have to suddenly start jogging. It is far better for you to ease yourself back into life at your own level of ability, without strain. If you are worried, check with your doctor before embarking on an exercise programme, especially if you are on medication or having treatment of any kind. By using a carefully graded exercise system that is also recreational, lots of fun, and preferably with musical accompaniment, you can be eased back into the flow of life.

And it is not just the physical side that will improve; the effects spill into your brain, spirit and emotions. Think of a square with the healthy 'whole you' in the middle – healthy because each

These are a few of the remarks made by men and women who have attended EXTEND classes. The main aim of the classes is to improve the quality of life for the over 60s, and the main tools are movement, music, fun and lots of laughter – the best tonic of all. Members all declare that gardening, walking, dancing and a host of other activities are enjoyed so much more because of increased mobility and improved circulation.

You do not have to go to classes, of course. There is an exercise booklet and tape you can use in your own home, or bathroom. Yes, it is amazing what you can do even in the bath! Next time you are having a soothing bath (preferably while someone else is in the house) do a few gentle movements: flex to your toes to give them a brush instead of bringing them up to you (but always gently); try a stretch by taking hold of the flannel diagonally and cornerwise, behind your back, holding corner-ends in each hand, one over the shoulder and one up the back, and then really move that flannel up and down. And swop to the other side. These movements are mobilizing and stimulating.

After your bath, really rub yourself dry, sitting down if necessary – this is not only invigorating, but it also disposes of dead skin and afterwards your body will tingle and glow. Then have a stretch up with your arms to the ceiling, keeping your chin in line with your spine to prevent dizziness; you should feel full of zest and ready to go.

Posture and balance also become increasingly important as we get older. Professor Bernard Isaacs, from the Department of Geriatrics at the University of Birmingham, believes that here, too, exercise can help, and may possibly reduce the number of falls and accidents that older people often have to be admitted to hospital for.

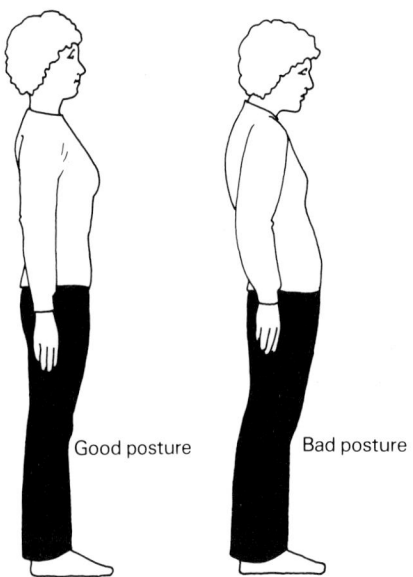

Good posture   Bad posture

Many exercises can be done sitting down. Try some of these, using music with a jolly 4/time beat.

Sit in an upright chair (if your feet dangle, place a support, such as a telephone directory, underneath them).

For the ankles
Clasp hands under right knee and straighten the leg. Point foot down, count 2, push heel out, bringing foot up, count 2. Do this four times and repeat with the other foot.

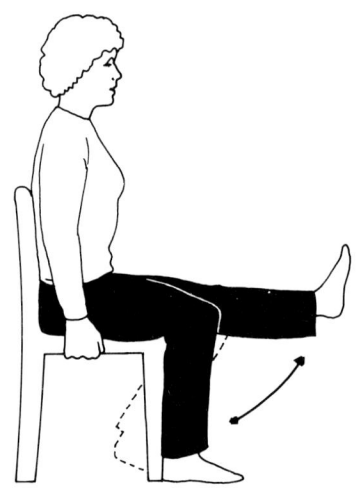

Exercising the knee

For the knees
Keeping knees together, swing right leg forward, until it is straight, count 1, swing it back under the chair, count 2. Do this six times, and repeat with left leg.

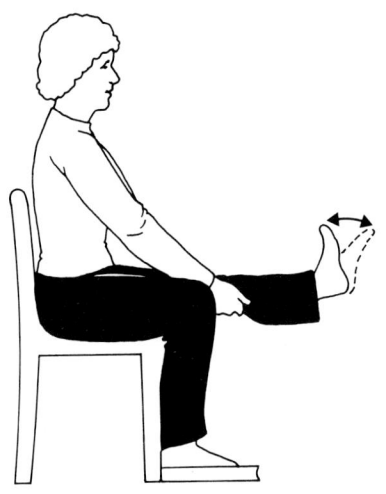

Exercising the ankle

For the hips

Clasp hands together under right knee and steadily pull thigh up, count 1; pull higher, count 2; and higher still, count 3; replace leg down on count 4. Do this four times, and repeat with other leg.

Try and maintain good, upright posture throughout.

That is just a small selection of exercises that will help mobilize and strengthen the joints and muscles in ankles, knees and hips and help to ensure a safer style of walking.

But do not just think of exercise as something you do once a day, or once a week, at home or in classes. Aim to keep warm by promoting your body circulation with warming-up exercises, by correct breathing, and make sure, too that you enjoy a good diet. Finally, make sure that everything you do around the house uses your body and muscles to the full. For instance, when I am doing the hoovering, I try to push the cleaner a few extra inches; when I do the washing up or ironing, I always try to pull in my tummy, tighten my seat and lift my ribs. When I hang out the washing, I breathe in deeply as I stretch up to the line. And when I lift any loads, I think about bending from the knees; at least I try to, because I know that otherwise I may lose that 'Get Up and Go' feeling, which could easily lead to blues, lethargy and stagnation. How about you? For more information, send a stamped, addressed envelope to:

EXTEND,
5 Conway Road,
Sheringham,
Norfolk NR26 9DD.
For the EXTEND exercise booklet send 75p (incl. postage and packing), and for musical cassette tape to exercises, send £3.75 (also incl. postage and packing).

One way of combining exercise with relaxation is to take up yoga. Even if you no longer have to cope with the stress of a full-time job, there are likely to be other areas of anxiety and yoga can be really useful in helping you unwind.

There are several organizations who specialize in yoga classes for older people. You can either write to the addresses below, enclosing a s.a.e., or check with your local adult education centre, which may include yoga in its schedule of classes.

Yoga For Health Foundation is a national organization. It runs a residential centre and eighty local clubs and centres throughout Britain. Their instructors will arrange courses either individually or in groups.
Yoga For Health Foundation,
Ickwell Bury,
Biggleswade,
Bedfordshire SG18 9EF.   phone: Northill 271 076 271

Iyengar Yoga Institute runs its own centres. In addition, many of its teachers run classes in conjunction with local education institutes.
Iyengar Yoga Institute,
95 Inchmerry Road,
London SE26.
The Edinburgh Iyengar Institute,
85 Spottiswood Street,
Edinburgh EH9 1NZ.

Sivananda Yoga Vedanta Centre holds classes for retired people, but will also send teachers to pensioners groups (free of charge) to give demonstration classes.
Sivananda Yoga Vedanta Centre,
50 Chepstow Villas,
London W11.   phone: 01-229-7970

Sport

If you thought that sport in retirement was restricted to an occasional session of shove ha'penny or a gentle game of bowls (in fact, a much underrated sport) you are probably in for a shock. Speedboat-racing grannies, like Lady Arran, and marathon-running grandads (there are now too many to mention) have put paid to that.

In 1983 The Sports Council launched a new campaign '50+ and All to Play For'. A quick browse through their leaflets makes it clear that there are no sports which are out of bounds for older people. And the emphasis is always on *enjoying yourself*. Before you write yourself off as 'not the sporting type' (probably because you

Lady Arran being interviewed on Years Ahead.

hated netball or cricket at school), have a look at the prospectus at your local education institute or sports centre to see what is available at day and evening sessions.

The English Tourist Board's book, *Activity and Hobby Holidays in England*, is also packed with names and addresses of centres that combine a holiday with a variety of sporting activities – everything from ballooning to wind-surfing.

Even if you really are not fit enough to take part in a vigorous sport that you once enjoyed, there is always a shortage of helpers (somebody has to organize the coaches for the away game, not to mention making the cucumber sandwiches). In this way, you can still share the friendly social atmosphere associated with your particular game.

Some local authorities organize sporting clubs with a variety of titles such as Over Fifties Fun Clubs, 60+ Keep Fit, and so on. The great advantage here is that even if you are already, say, a squash fanatic, you can use the courts at reduced rates and you can try your hand at some activities you may not have considered before.

Undoubtedly, one of the best we have heard of is the centre at Alton, in Hampshire.

Croquet is a sport that you can continue to participate in well into old age.

The Health and Fun Club for the over fifty-fives was set up eight years ago. Since then, it has proved so popular that they not only have a display team – beautifully attired in maroon leotards – to advise groups in other areas, but they have also had to put on extra classes each week.

For just £6 a year + 75p for each day they attend, members get the run of the club and use of most of the facilities completely free. There are so many to choose from: two levels of keep fit, old-time dancing, squash, badminton, bowls, and swimming in the luxurious heated pool.

The social side of the club is very active too, with excursions and group holidays.

When we went down to Alton to film, we found the atmosphere there really infectious – so many people laughing, enjoying themselves and getting so much out of life.

Perhaps the outstanding success story at Alton is Kay Rogers. Fifteen years ago Kay was a progressive arthritic, declared unfit for work by a panel of doctors. As she puts it: 'I was shuffling round at home and getting so depressed – feeling so old.' She decided to try out a diet she had heard about, based on codliver oil, and after a few months began to notice quite an improvement. So much so she joined the keep fit group at Alton, joining in the few exercises she could manage, gently at first.

'Before I knew it, bingo, I was doing the whole thing,' she says, now beaming with health. Kay has become part of the display team at Alton, and her involvement with the group was a great comfort when she lost her husband a year ago. 'Everyone rallied round to help me through,' she says, 'and having responsibilities within the group really helped me so much. I knew I couldn't let them down.'

The Sports Council,
16 Upper Woburn Place,
London WC1.   phone: 01-388-1277

Alton Sports Centre,
Alton,
Hampshire.

English Tourist Board, *Activity and Hobby Holidays in England*, £1.25

Kay Rogers's Diet
1 tablespoon of orange juice or milk
1 tablespoon of codliver oil
Shake to mix well.
This mixture to be taken daily on an empty stomach, either one hour before breakfast or last thing at night, three hours after last meal or drink.

After six months, dosage can be reduced to every other day. This combined with the diet should start to reduce pain after about six weeks.

Forbidden foods
Butter (use polyunsaturated margarine instead)
White bread (use brown)
White sugar (use brown)
Citrus fruits (oranges, lemons, plums)
Tomatoes
Cream, cream cakes, ice cream
Cheese can be used in moderation
One egg per week
No meat except poultry
An attempt should be made to minimize all monosodium glutomate, so read labels on tins, etc., very carefully.

No fizzy drinks and no alcohol, except an occasional whisky and soda.

One other irritating rule: no coffee or tea until at least one hour after a meal.
Lastly, *no pepper*.

Suitable foods
All kinds of fish
All kinds of vegetables and salads, except tomatoes
All kinds of nuts (except salted)

When cooking, use vegetable oil rather than animal fats and always grill rather than fry.

Potatoes should be baked in their jackets or mashed, never roasted in fat. This may all seem very restricting, but good planning can make it more interesting.

How to use the NHS

Your first point of contact within the National Health Service is likely to be your:

GENERAL PRACTITIONER (GP)

If you do not already have a GP, or have moved to a new area, you need to register with one straight-away. Names and addresses of doctors in the area will be available from the Citizens' Advice Bureau, the post office or library, but best of all is to ask around among friends and see who they go to. If you already have a GP but are not happy with the service you are getting, you could try going to another doctor in that practice, or you could change altogether. Nothing could be simpler: all you do is write a letter to the Family Practitioner Committee (for England and Wales) the Central Services Agency (for Northern Ireland) or the local Health Board (Scotland) explaining that you wish to change and enclosing your medical card. You do not have to give a reason, and it is the duty of the Committee or Board to make sure that you are not left without a GP.

If you feel strongly that you have been badly treated by your doctor, write a letter setting out your complaints to the appropriate Board or Committee. They will look into the matter. You should write within eight weeks (six in Scotland and Northern Ireland) of the incident that has upset you.

If you feel your doctor has behaved in an unprofessional or unethical manner, for example, charging for free services or propositioning you, complain in writing to:

General Medical Council,
44 Hallam Street,
London W1.

General Medical Council,
8 Queen Street,
Edinburgh.

You can also help your doctor to help you by phoning the surgery before 10 am, particularly if you need a home visit. Make a list of any symptoms you have and take it to the surgery with you; it is easy to forget otherwise. If you are visiting him about more than one illness, again make a list so you do not forget anything. If he prescribes pills for you, take them. If you feel they do not agree with you, tell him why you have stopped taking them. If you feel you would like a second opinion, ask your doctor about making an appointment with a specialist. If he refuses to do this, the only option is to change your GP.

Your doctor's surgery should also be able to advise you if you need the services of: a health visitor (general advice on health problems); district nursing sister (for home nursing help); social worker, physiotherapist or dietician.

HOSPITALS

It is very easy to feel worried if you go to visit someone in hospital. All the efforts of the staff are put into making the patient well, and if you are observing a loved one from the sidelines it can give rise to all manner of anxieties, often unnecessarily.

If you genuinely feel that either you, or a close relative, is not getting the care or treatment needed, first try talking to the medical staff – a senior member of the nursing staff or the consultant. If the situation does not change there are several steps you can take:

If your complaint is about hospital services and organization, dirty wards, or a very long wait for an operation, write to the Hospital or District Administrator. If that produces no acceptable solution, contact *The Ombudsman* (see below).

If, on the other hand, your grievance is a medical one, you should write to your local area health authority.

STILL NOT SATISFIED?

There are various bodies to help you.
Community Health Councils have offices throughout England and Wales (in Scotland they are called Local Health Councils and in Northern Ireland, District Committees). Their job is to advise you about the services of both GPs and hospitals in the area, and to help if you want to make an official complaint about either, including how to complain to *The Ombudsman*.

Patients Association,
11 Dartmouth Street,
London SW1H 9BN.   phone: 01-222-4992
(Runs an advice service for patients)

Do not be afraid to complain if you are dissatisfied with your treatment or feel something is not right. By bringing the matter to light, you could be saving someone else from a similar experience.

Health: who to ask for help

ARTHRITIS
This is a disease, not just a manifestation of old age. If you have painful joints or stiff fingers, see your doctor.

Arthritis Care,
6 Grosvenor Crescent,
London SW1X 7ER.

Lorig, K. & Fries, J. F., *The Arthritis Helpbook*, (Souvenir Press, 1983) £8.95.

BACK PAIN
This is suffered by four out of five people at some point in their lives, often caused by bad posture. Can sometimes be helped by 'alternative therapies', such as acupuncture or osteopathy. Unless you are lucky enough to live near the few centres that provide this on the NHS, you will have to go privately.

The Back Pain Association,
31-33 Park Road,
Teddington,
Middlesex.
Devlin, Dr D., *You and Your Back Pain*, (The Back Pain Association), £1.20.

DEPRESSION
Depression often sets in following bereavement. In addition to the symptoms of grief, you may feel unbearably tired, anxious and unable to sleep. Here your doctor really can help if you explain things to him.

Depressives Anonymous,
Self-Help Centre,
83 Derby Road,
Nottingham NG1 5BB.
Have a number of self-help groups throughout Britain.

EXCESSIVE DRINKING
This often goes hand in hand with depression (see above) but only provides a temporary solution. Many people drink more after a bereavement, which is fine so long as it is just a short passing phase. Many doctors now agree alcohol *in moderation* does no harm at all, but only you can decide if you have a drinking problem (often the hardest part). Talk things over with your doctor or get in touch with Alcoholics Anonymous – the number is in the phone book.

EYES
If your eyesight is not as good as it used to be, ask at your local optician's for an eye test, which is *free*. He may suggest glasses (which are free to those receiving supplementary pension). Poor lighting can sometimes be the cause of the problem, and this can easily be rectified. Many other eye problems can also be treated successfully – *provided* they are diagnosed early on by a qualified optician. For the small minority who do become blind, the RNIB can provide talking books, talking newspapers and various other forms of help.

The Royal National Institute for the Blind,
224 Great Portland Street,
London W1N 6AA.   phone: 01-388-1266

FEET
If your feet are not in good condition, they can totally wreck your chances of enjoying retirement. You should make sure that:
you wear good fitting shoes; you wash (but do not soak) your feet regularly; dry them well, rubbing in a little cream if the skin feels dry; use cotton buds to get between the toes; cut your nails regularly straight across, using a nail clipper if you find this easier; *do not* use corn plasters – skin gets thinner with age and you could end up with a nasty 'burn'.

Check with the doctor to see if there is a community chiropody service near you or, alternatively, some branches of *Age Concern* organize a nail-cutting service.

HEARING

Some difficulty in hearing *may* arise through 'natural wear and tear', or it may be due to something more specific. *Do not* take any chances; check with your doctor. It could even be that your ears need syringing to clear them of wax. Even if it is more serious, there are a lot of sophisticated hearing aids available, and other forms of help such as inductive loops (to enable you to enjoy television without having the set turned up very loud), and the very successful Sympathetic Hearing Scheme – signs displayed in a number of shops show that they appreciate the difficulties deaf people have and know how to deal with them. Many social services departments also have special social workers for the deaf with specific knowledge on lip-reading classes.

The Royal National Institute for the Deaf,
105 Gower Street,
London WC1E 6AH.   phone: 01-387-8033

Mr Clive Palmer,
Secretary,
National Council of Social Workers for the Deaf,
c/o Redbridge Social Services,
17/23 Clements Road,
Ilford,
Essex IG1 1BL.

The Sympathetic Hearing Scheme,
7-11 Armstrong Road,
London W3 7JL.   phone: 01-743-1110

ATLA Information,
c/o The Post Office,
Slimbridge,
Gloucester.
For details of lip-reading classes.

INCONTINENCE

This is a problem that affects a great number of people at one time or another. Get help, in the form of disposable pads, special clothing and a number of other aids – some of which will be free of charge, some you will have to pay for. Try and get the help of a specialist 'Continence Advisor'. If there is not one in your area, contact the district nurse, health visitor, or your doctor.

Incontinence: A Guide to the Understanding and Management of a Very Common Complaint, Disabled Living Foundation, £4.10 inc. p&p.

DEMENTIA

The two most common causes of dementia are Alzheimers Disease (more often found in women than in men), and arteriosclerosis, hardening of the arteries, which affects more men than women. The symptoms include forgetfulness, restlessness and disorientation. If you notice that someone is becoming confused over a number of days or weeks check up first on his or her physical state – the confusion may be caused by an imbalanced diet or some other condition which will respond to treatment. Looking after someone with dementia places an enormous burden on the carer, so make sure you get all the help that is available before the strain makes you ill too. The social services department may be able to help in a number of ways; there will also be allowances that you are entitled to claim. Write to any of the addresses below for further information.

Alzheimers Disease Society (ADS),
Third Floor,
Bank Buildings,
Fulham Broadway,
London SW6 1EP.   phone 01-381-3177

ADS Office,
67 York Place,
Edinburgh EH1 3JD.   phone: 031-556-3062

Crossroads Care Attendant Schemes,
94a Coton Road,
Rugby,
Warwickshire CV21 4LN.

or 24 George Square,
Glasgow G2.

or The Co-Ordinator,
Bryson House,
28 Bedford St,
Belfast BT2 7FJ.

STROKES

A stroke is caused by an interruption in the supply of blood to the brain. This disturbs the functioning of some part of the brain. It can be so slight that it is not noticed, or severe enough to cause paralysis on one side, loss of speech or a distortion of the face.

Rehabilitation is often a long process, but there will be a whole team of people to help the patient regain their abilities and overcome the feelings of frustration and loneliness that often follow a stroke.

Chest, Heart and Stroke Association,
Tavistock House North,
Tavistock Square,
London WC1H 9JF.

Chest, Heart and Stroke Association,
65 North Castle Street,
Edinburgh EH2 3LT.

Chest, Heart and Stroke Association,
28 Bedford Street,
Belfast BT2 7FJ.

Other useful addresses:
Disabled Living Foundation,
Information Services,
346 Kensington High Street,
London W14 8NS.

Royal Association for Disability and Rehabilitation (RADAR),
25 Mortimer Steet,
London W1N 8AB.

National Association of Carers,
58 New Road,
Chatham,
Kent ME4 4QR.

ALTERNATIVE MEDICINE

This term covers a wide range of therapies, some of which may be available on the National Health. If your GP does not offer any of them, ask to be referred to another practitioner; for example, if you want homoeopathy, you could be referred to one of the five regional homoeopathic hospitals, in London, Bristol, Liverpool, Glasgow and Tunbridge Wells. With many of the complementary or alternative therapies, however, you may have to pay for private treatment.

There is an excellent new consumers' guide which gives a no-nonsense account of what is involved in each of the therapies that make up alternative or complementary medicine.

Inglis, B. & West, R., *The Alternative Health Guide*, (Michael Joseph, 1983), £12.50.

Food and diet

Staying healthy is of prime importance in order to get the most out of being retired – whatever your plans are – and this means among other things, paying attention to what you eat. In addition, the cost of the food you buy must be taken into account. Food is frequently the biggest item of expenditure for retired people. Most people living on a pension spend between a quarter and a third of it on buying things to eat. Even if you shop carefully it is difficult to keep the cost down, when the prices of most foods keep on going up.

For our *Years Ahead* cooking section, we asked nutritionist **Patty Fisher** and chef **Kenneth Toyé** to come up with a *Years Ahead Shopping Basket*, which must not only include all the item necessary for a well-balanced diet, but it must also cost not more than £10.50. Quite a daunting challenge? Well you can see the results of their efforts on page 79, and perhaps use their list as a guide, varying certain items from time to time, according to your own preferences.

What are the basic groups of foods that must be included?
Protein for body-building (fish, meat, cheese, eggs, beans, peas, bread, milk, nuts).
Calcium and phosphorous for strong bones and teeth (yogurt, cheese, milk and bread).
Vitamin A for skin and eyes (oily fish, carrots, tomatoes, dark green vegetables and dairy products).
B Vitamins for muscular energy (liver, heart, kidney, yeast, flour, bread, oats, cereals, peas, beans, potatoes, milk and cheese).
Vitamin C for connective tissues and resistance to infection (citrus fruits, berries, melon, green

leaf vegetables, cauliflower, cress, salad vegetables and tomatoes, rosehip syrup).

Vitamin D to help the body absorb calcium (halibut liver oil capsules, margarine, butter, meat, cheese, egg yolk).

Iron for making red blood for vitality (red meats, eggs, flour, bread, bran, offal).

Dietary fibre, or roughage, for gut health (bran, whole grain cereals, wholemeal bread).

Because so many foods we buy today are processed and over refined, additional fibre, in the form of bran and cereals (or even vegetables such as celery) are very important if you want to avoid digestive problems and constipation. It is a sad fact that as a race we were by and large *healthier* during the war years when butter, fats, sugar, sweets and so on, were in such short supply. Cut down too, if you can, on salt – sometimes a few drops of lemon juice are a pleasant alternative as a seasoning.

A few more tips to keep your shopping bill down:

– Never go shopping on an empty stomach, you will end up buying more than you need.

– Buy seasonal fruit and vegetables when they are plentiful.

– Larger amounts cost less – but only if it is something which keeps.

– Take your own shopping bag with you to save buying endless carriers.

– Shop around – prices can vary enormously from store to store.

– 'Own brands' are usually cheaper than familiar names (and often made by the same company).

– Supermarkets (especially the big ones) sell perishable foods cheaply at the end of the day and before the weekend.

– Make a friend of the butcher. By asking his advice and going to him regularly he will not mind if you ask for a couple of rashers of bacon or bones for stock.

– Order your milk and/or bread, eggs and so on through the milkman. There is a real danger that if milk rounds become uneconomic they will gradually die out, and no one wants that.

Do not throw away herbs, such as parsley,

when you have to buy more than you need. Instead, chop it up and place in an ice cube tray with enough water to cover and freeze. When you want to use it pop the cube in a tea strainer and run under the cold tap. The parsley will not be so crisp, but it will be green and fresh.

When using the oven, cook two or three dishes at the same time to make the most of the fuel. For boiled or steamed food, a pressure cooker is more economical than a saucepan.

Soy sauce is made from fermented soya beans, and it is a cheaper and better alternative to stock cubes, and healthier. Try and get real Chinese or Japanese soy sauce, which is much better than British imitations.

Cool leftover food as quickly as possible, and reheat thoroughly before eating. Never reheat food until it is just warm, in order to save fuel – make sure it is really hot all the way through, or you may risk food poisoning.

Buy a cheap photo album (with the peel-back, clear pages) in which to keep the recipes you cut out of papers or magazines. This way the recipes stay clean; and you throw them out if you become bored with them.

The Years Ahead *Shopping Basket contains all the ingredients needed for a well-balanced and nutritious diet, at a very economical price.*

YEARS AHEAD SHOPPING BASKET

A week's healthy and economical food for one person.

2 chicken portions (12 oz)	87p	
4oz liver	14p	
4 oz ham loaf or sliced sausage	33p	
4oz heart	24p	
8oz tripe	31p	
12oz cheddar cheese	93p	
4 eggs	26p	
4oz bacon pieces	10p	
8oz smoked mackerel fillets (or pilchards)	54p	(29p)
1lb butter beans (or 15 oz tin baked beans)	57p	(17½p)
3½oz dried milk powder	22½p	
14oz tin evaporated milk	27½p	
1lb plain flour	25p	
8oz porridge oats	20p	
8oz semi-sweet biscuits	18½p	
8oz sugar	12p	
1 packet jelly cubes	13p	
4oz treacle	11p	
4oz tea	29½p	
1 packet soup powder	27½p	
14oz fresh or tinned tomatoes	19p	
4oz sunflower oil	20½p	
8oz low-fat margarine	32½p	
4oz unprocessed bran	9½p	
6 meat extract cubes	16½p	
1 small loaf of bread	28p	
1 large loaf of bread	35p	
1lb onions	22p	
1lb carrots	20p	
1 red pepper (capsicum)	15p	
1lb of rice or pasta	39p	
7oz rosehip syrup	59p	
10 halibut liver oil capsules	9p	
3 pints of fresh milk	61½p	
4oz butter	23p	
Seasonings (salt, pepper, herbs, garlic)	5p	

£10.80½p or

(£10.16½p)

The prices shown on the Shopping Basket are what we paid in a supermarket in September 1983. They will probably have risen since then, particularly seasonal items.

We have chosen the cheapest sources of different nutrients. Of course, you can buy steak instead of heart and tripe, and orange juice instead of rosehip syrup, but they will cost more and their food value is no higher.

We also asked **Kenneth Toyé** to come up with a selection of recipes that are very simple and that do not take a long while to cook. The most sensible plan is to cook a good nourishing casserole gently in the oven for several hours, but if you are on your own, so often it becomes a case of 'I can't be bothered'. Then you get hungry and grab a cheese sandwich – hardly the basis of a healthy, well-balanced diet.

Kenneth Toyé, the Years Ahead *chef, has provided a selection of nourishing recipes that are simple and quick to cook (see pages 80-1).*

YEARS AHEAD RECIPES
Succotash (for one)

1/3 teacup dried butter (Lima) beans
1 small onion
1 small red pepper
2 tablespoons sweetcorn
1 tablespoon vegetable oil
1 small clove garlic (optional)
2 teaspoons butter
2 teaspoons plain flour
½ pint milk
1 tablespoon grated cheddar cheese
salt and pepper

Soak the beans overnight. Cook them in slightly salted water until they are soft.

Chop the onion and the red pepper, place them in a pan, with the sweetcorn; and fry in a little oil until soft. Add chopped garlic (if used), salt and pepper to flavour.

Melt the butter in a saucepan and add the flour, then cook this paste for two minutes over a very low heat. Warm the milk and add it gradually to the paste, stirring all the time. Add the grated cheese to the sauce, and add salt and pepper to taste.

Serve the beans, onion and pepper onto a warm plate, and pour the cheese sauce over the top. Serve with warm, crusty bread to soak up the delicious juices.

Chicken Spanish Style (for one)

½ teacup uncooked brown rice
4 oz portion cooked chicken
1 small onion
1 fresh tomato or 1 small tin tomatoes
1 tablespoon vegetable oil
pinch of dried mixed herbs
1 small clove garlic (optional)
½ teacup leftover cooked vegetables
1 tablespoon grated cheese (optional)
salt and pepper

Pre-cook the rice in twice its volume (1 teacup) of lightly salted water in a covered pan until all the water is absorbed (about 40 minutes for brown rice). If your chicken portion is uncooked, fry it gently in a little oil for about 15 minutes.

Chop the onion and skin the tomato (if using a fresh one) by placing it in a cup of very hot water. Fry the onion and tomato (or tinned tomatoes) in a little of the vegetable oil. Add the mixed herbs and garlic (if used).

Place the cooked chicken on top of this mixture and heat it through thoroughly. Add the cooked rice and half a teacup of water to the pan and simmer, sprinkling the cooked leftover vegetables (if used) over the top.

Check the flavour and season with salt and pepper to taste. If desired, grate a little cheese over the dish just before serving on a warm plate or dish.

Mackerel North Channel Style (for one)

1 small onion
1 dessertspoon vegetable oil
1 fresh, skinned tomato or small tin tomatoes, chopped
dried mixed herbs or basil
½ cup uncooked pasta shapes
¼ lb smoked mackerel fillet
1 tablespoon grated cheese
salt and pepper

Chop the onion and fry in a pan with some oil. Add chopped tomatoes from a tin or a skinned fresh tomato. Add herbs and season to taste, add a little water and simmer.

Next, cook the pasta in lightly salted boiling water until it just begins to soften. (A drop of oil in the boiling water will stop the pasta sticking). Drain.

Skin the smoked mackerel fillet, and place in a pan with a little water. Simmer until heated through.

To serve, pile the pasta on a warm plate. Add the tomato sauce, sprinkle with cheese and place the hot mackerel beside it.

Liver with Braised Cabbage (for one)

2 small potatoes
1 medium onion
8 oz shredded cabbage
1 dessertspoon vinegar
6 oz ox liver
1 teaspoon flour
1 dessertspoon vermouth, sherry, port or marsala
a few white grapes (optional)
salt and pepper

Scrub the potatoes and boil them in their skins in salted water until soft.

Meanwhile, chop the onion and fry gently in a saucepan. Chop the cabbage and mix with the onion. Pour in the vinegar and a little water. Season to taste, and simmer gently until the onion starts to soften – the cabbage should still be quite crisp.

Dust the liver with flour and fry in a little hot oil in a frying pan. When cooked (about five minutes later) sprinkle with sweet vermouth, sherry, port or marsala. If using grapes, cut them in half, discard the pips and add to the sauce to simmer.

Serve the liver garnished with the cabbage and potatoes, topped with the vermouth sauce.

Smoked Herring Pâté (for two)

1 medium-sized fillet of smoked herring (or mackerel)
3 oz butter and margarine mixed
juice of a small lemon

Skin the fish and mash with a fork.

Add the butter and margarine and work to a paste. Mix in the lemon juice. Set in a small bowl in the fridge.

Serve on toast slices. Eat with a cucumber salad.

Marinades

A good way of making money stretch further is by buying relatively inexpensive cuts of meat and marinating them. This means soaking the meat in a cold liquid – a marinade – for several hours before you cook it. According to which marinade you use, this will give the meat extra flavour and break down some of the fibres in the meat, making it more tender.

Here is a very simple marinade, suitable for those frozen chicken pieces that often seem to have no flavour of their own:

Mix together (for one):
½ clove of garlic, chopped or crushed
juice of one lemon
peel of one lemon, chopped up, and with all the white pith removed
1 tablespoon of oil (olive if possible)
1 tablespoon of soy sauce

Pour into a shallow fireproof dish and add the defrosted chicken piece, flesh down. Spoon the marinade over the chicken, pressing the lemon peel into the flesh. Leave to soak for at least 2 hours, basting with the liquid occasionally. You can then either grill the chick-en, still in the fireproof pan, or fry it, pouring a tablespoon or two of the marinade over the chicken as it cooks. Check whether it is cooked by inserting a sharp knife into the chicken – the juices will run clear if it is cooked, pink if it needs longer. Serve with rice or pasta and a green salad.

Clafoutis (light sponge)

1 tablespoon plain flour
½ tablespoon gran. sugar
pinch of salt
1 egg (medium)
½ teaspoon mixed spice
¼ pt milk
½ cooking apple (peeled and sliced) or similar quantity of other fruit

In a bowl, mix flour, sugar, salt, egg and mixed spice. Stir in the milk to make a runny batter.

Grease a small ovenproof dish (½ pt size). Arrange fruit in the bottom and pour mixture into the dish. Bake in a moderate oven for about 30 minutes, until well risen and golden brown.

Serve with remaining sliced apple or other fruit.

Eve's Pudding (for four)

sponge
2 oz sugar
2 oz margarine
2 oz self-raising flour
pinch of salt
2 eggs (medium)
milk to mix
filling
2 large cooking apples
2 tablespoons sugar
1 teaspoon mixed spice
juice of half a lemon

Cream sugar and margarine until light and fluffy. Gradually beat in the eggs and a little flour. Sift flour and salt into the mixture, and fold it in. Add milk if necessary to make a soft dropping mixture.

Peel and slice apples. Arrange in a 7 in medium-sized pie dish. Sprinkle sugar and spice over the apples, and add lemon juice. Spread sponge mixture over top to cover the apples. Bake in oven 180°C for 45-60 minutes, until sponge is golden brown and well risen.

LUNCH CLUBS

Cooking for one can seem a waste of time, and often you do not want to eat on your own either. So lunch clubs are a good way of combining meals with the opportunity to meet people. If you do not have a local lunch club why not set one up yourself? If you get a few friends together you can take it in turn to cook, and eat at each other's houses in rotation; or if there are lots of you, your lunch club could be held in the local hall.

Even if you do not want to cook, or find it difficult, it may be possible to organize meals on wheels for all your lunch club to be delivered at the same place. That way you still enjoy some conversation and companionship with your food. Contact: the social services department at your local council.

MEALS ON WHEELS

While the standards and prices of meals on wheels vary enormously, the principle is always the same. If a person is housebound and unable to cook for himself, or to get a relative or neighbour to cook for him, the local council will provide meals on wheels.

The food may be bought by the council pre-packaged, and then simply heated up and delivered, or it may be cooked specially by WRVS volunteers, or bought each day from a nearby school or works canteen and then taken round at lunchtime.

In some areas you can have a maximum of two meals delivered each week, other councils provide them every day. The price varies widely too: from as little as 39p in one London borough to

The meals on wheels service is run by local councils for people who are housebound, who are unable to cook for themselves and who have no relative or neighbour to cook for them.

90p in some counties, though in general the cost of providing the meal is considerably higher.

If you live in a city, there will probably be a choice of diets, and the range may include vegetarian, diabetic, low-fat, reducing, high-protein, soft and Asian. Special medical diets recommended by your doctor are available throughout the country and there are voluntary organizations which cater for special needs. The League of Jewish Women, for instance, provides kosher meals which are delivered in the same way as ordinary ones.

If you think you qualify for meals on wheels and you do not already receive them, contact your social services department through the council.

ENTERTAINING (ON YOUR OWN)

To have friends or family round for a meal can be one of life's greatest pleasures, but if you are accustomed to having a partner there to share the chores, trying to do it all on your own can change it into a nightmare. Here are a few ideas to help make it as painless as possible:

Do not bother with a first course, provide a few nibbles, cheese straws or nuts. This way you can sit and talk to people when they arrive instead of rushing out to the kitchen.

Empty the cubes out of the ice tray into a plastic bag and put back in the ice compartment of your fridge or freezer. You will have a plentiful, and accessible, supply of ice for drinks.

Do not be too ambitious! Stick to tried and trusted recipes.

Cook as much as possible in advance. A casserole, for instance, needs only to be taken out of the oven, and it will not be ruined if your guests are half an hour late. Jacket potatoes save you

work peeling, and will not spoil. A cold dessert can come straight from the fridge.

Keep a trolley or small table near where you are eating, which can be used for keeping plates and food on to save you trips to the kitchen.

BULK BUYING AND FOOD CO-OPS

Yet another way of cutting food costs is to buy in bulk. Often you can best do this by joining a local food co-op where members club together to share the benefits. In one typical co-op the members meet every week to put in their orders and to pick up the food they ordered the week before.

Every Friday they take it in turns to drive a van, supplied by the local council, down to the nearest fruit and vegetable market with their members' shopping list, and they get a discount for quantity. Every other week the shoppers go on to a nearby cash-and-carry store to buy the groceries. Back at the co-op meeting the same afternoon, the groceries, fruit and vegetables are shared out and paid for.

Once a month there is also a trip to a wholesale butcher for meat, which can be kept frozen until needed.

With a few dozen members, discounts for bulk will not be very high and without council assistance, in the shape of a van and possibly a driver, the savings may be small. But even so, the social element of a food co-op is often worth more than the financial benefit and there is a particular advantage for members who find it difficult or impossible to shop for themselves.

If you like the idea of a food co-op, check with the local council and Citizens' Advice Bureau to see whether there is one already operating in your area or for advice on setting up your own.

6 'But I'm too young to be an OAP'

Robert Dougall

The trouble with getting older is that we still basically feel much the same as we did when we were youngsters. It can come as a terrible shock to read a headline in a newspaper, 'Elderly man injured in road accident', only to discover this 'elderly man' is the same age as you! And what a variety of names there are for us too. Old age pensioner is bad enough but the euphemism 'senior citizen' is almost worse. One of the best suggestions we have received on *Years Ahead* came from Mr F. R. Figg of Luton, who said: 'I always use the words Ancient Briton. Whether they like it or not, when people hear this they always smile – and a smile is always worthwhile'.

Whatever we call ourselves, it can be quite a rude shock to discover how others see us. This was brought home to me a few years ago when, during a stay in Athens, Nan and I took the cable-car up the hill of Lycabettus. The car was crowded; Nan got a seat, but I was quite happy standing. After a minute or two I noticed a charming young girl sitting a few seats away – and, yes, she was definitely smiling at me, quite roguishly. I must admit I found this rather gratifying and I suppose I twinkled back at her a little and probably straightened my shoulders a bit too. Then, to my astonishment and horror, she rose and, of all things, asked me if I would like to sit down! I declined as graciously as possible – but what could be more deflating. As someone wisely said: 'Old is anyone ten years older than me.'

Despite all our suggestions in the previous pages on ways of keeping active, undoubtedly one of the joys of retirement is the luxury of a little time, just to sit and think, away from the 'treadmill' of a working routine. Time to take in some new ideas, to reflect on some old ones and simply to 'put your house in order'.

Ageism

Kay Sykes

Age is a measurement of life, just as feet and inches, and pounds and ounces, measure height and weight. We do not judge people by their height and weight so why do we make such a fuss about age? Ageing starts at birth, and the first question often asked is 'How old is he?' Ten days – ten weeks – ten years – one hundred years? Surely such precision is unnecessary and it is far better to assess people by their actions and intellect.

None of us like growing old, and society's attitude heightens this apprehension quite unnecessarily. As with all reporting, it is generally the bad side that is high-lighted, the pathetic, the handicapped, sad and lonely, rather than the run-of-the-mill types living their lives in a perfectly normal way. Why is it that if we who are over sixty continue to enjoy an active busy life, someone is bound to come up to us and say 'I don't know how you do it' (implying 'at your age'!). We have got out of the box they have mentally put us in and upset the image of the Retired Person, whatever that might be. Generalization is bad; it suits a computer very well, but we are human beings and will retain our individuality until the day we die. What gifts we had as young people are increased as we grow up – thank goodness nobody yet refers to 'growing down'!

Much lip service is paid to retired people by all political parties, but in the end we become an embarrassment to them – we are difficult to absorb into the labour market – and so it is easier to maintain that we are 'past it' at a certain age. Not so in the last war! Then those getting on for retirement were exhorted to continue, told how

Graham Stevens took up water ski-ing when he was fifty years old. Since then, he has won European and British Veteran's jumping championships. Now sixty, he trains twice weekly, and his ambition is to reach the 20 metre mark in ski-jumping events.

invaluable they were, and used to the full. My own father returned to work at the age of seventy and did not give up until the end of the war, when he was seventy five. Age did not matter then and it is a great loss that it cannot be the same now. Many people are late developers; they reach their peak much later in life than others. There is many an Open University graduate over sixty raring to go, and the popularity of the University of the Third Age tells us the same tale.

Possibly the rush of modern living has much to do with the impatience felt with older people. With everyone dashing to the next appointment, we seem to have lost the art of listening, finding out what people have achieved, what they have to offer. And this is a pity because so often it is the young who are the losers.

Let us try and get rid of ageism – such an ugly word that we could well do without it. In the United States there is a militant group of pensioners called 'The Grey Panthers'. They feel so strongly about ageism that if they see something on television or in the newspapers which they feel is unfair they bombard the manufacturer or TV channel and demand that it is taken off. You may not want to go quite that far, but if you see an advertisement that really irritates you, why not write to the advertiser or the Advertising Standards Authority? Get your friends to do the same. And the next time somebody uses the word geriatric as an adjective synonymous with 'old' or 'old-fashioned', ask them what it means.

We know the fuss about age is nonsense – let us make sure everyone else does too!

The Pensioners' Movement

Ethel Chipchase

People give us a variety of names from the day we are born. First, babies; then schoolchildren; now suddenly, we are variously called old age pensioners, senior citizens, the retired, the elderly, or just pensioners.

But whatever the name, there are some ten million of us – more than one in five of the population is of retirement age. And, of course, as with every other section of the community, we are a mixed bunch. We have different backgrounds, different circumstances. Some of us, fortunately, are still financially comfortable and in good health, and for us the years of retirement may well be the best years of our lives.

Once we retire, we do all have one thing in common. Whilst we remain the same people, the

Ethel Chipchase.

environment suddenly changes. It is like a migration to an unknown land. Problems can no longer be resolved through discussion and negotiation with management; there can be no threat of collective action in a dispute; we have no labour to withdraw. Within a single day the protection of the work environment, the union or the professional association is withdrawn.

WHY DO WE NEED A PENSIONERS' MOVEMENT?

You may have decided, having read the advice and help on the preceding pages, that the next few years will be relaxed and happy ones – and, indeed, many of us in the Movement would rather spend more time cultivating our gardens, or out and about doing the things we never had time for before.

But it is a sad fact of life that for many thousands of people, the later years bring financial hardship, failing health and loneliness. The majority of the elderly are women, the majority of those with only the state pension on which to live are women, the majority of the three-and-a-half million elderly who live alone are women. We cannot sit back whilst thousands – perhaps millions – of fellow pensioners exist on only a state pension which does not even allow them sufficient to heat their homes properly or to afford decent food.

There are many other issues too: the increasingly rapid rises in standing charges on gas and electricity. Even health is jeopardized. Pensioners are the biggest users of the National Health services, and it is those services which pensioners use most, which are at greatest risk under the present stringent cuts. Not only hospital services are threatened. Pensioners needing chiropody, which should be free to them, may be advised to 'go private' because they may otherwise wait up to a year before receiving attention. You must have noticed, reading through this book, how often the local authority decides what help is available for retired people, depending on where you live. The Pensioners' Movement believes that free local transport, to encourage mobility, and reduced television licences should be available to *all*.

In March each year, pensioners from all over the country gather at Westminster for the National Pensioners Convention.

HOW DID THE MOVEMENT START?

A few years ago there were a number of organizations helping the most disadvantaged to obtain the allowances and assistance then available. In many cases the men and women involved became angry and militant as they saw the pensioners' situation deteriorate, but they were not designed to be pioneering pressure groups and it was feared this might lead to political conflict.

At that particular time the TUC had enough to do dealing with the problems of their current members, but as a few active trade unionists themselves reached retirement age they put their considerable experience and energy into forming organizations to promote the interests of all pensioners. Notable among these is Jack Jones who, when he retired from the Transport and General Workers Union in 1978, founded an association for retired members of that union. The Association has the support of the TGWU and every month its journal devotes a page to pensioners' issues.

Not all unions, however, were willing or able to do as much for their retired members. So Fred Baker helped found the British Pensioners and Trade Union Action Association (BPTUAA) to fill this gap. This Association is open to all retired trade union members and their families.

In 1979, the TUC got together with a number of pensioner groups and co-ordinated the first National Pensioners' Convention, which now takes place every year at the beginning of March.

It consists of a mass meeting in Central Hall, Westminster, followed by a lobby of Parliament. Its object is to improve the quality of life of retired people, and the Convention's members include charities, pressure groups and community and trade-union-based organizations.

The Convention formulated a Declaration of Intent, which starts with the statement that: 'Every pensioner should have the right to choice, dignity, independence and security as an integral and valued member of society.' The Declaration also lists ten demands, which include an adequate pension, accommodation appropriate to personal need, substantial concessionary travel facilities, the ability to maintain a warm and well-lit home, and an adequate death grant.

In addition to the BPTUAA there is The National Federation of Old Age Pensioners, now known as Pensioners' Voice, which is 'non-party and non-sectarian', with branches throughout the country, and it also holds an annual conference.

Jack Jones says that The Pensioners' Movement is a broad front. Just as the various religions in Britain now work closely together, so do the strands of The Pensioners' Movement. If more of us worked together, instead of being ten million isolated individuals, we could become the single most important pressure group in the country. And while there is a single pensioner not treated with the respect due to those who have worked throughout their lives – up to half a century – The Pensioners' Movement will continue, no matter what Government is in power at Westminster.

National Pensioners Convention,
c/o Trades Union Congress,
Congress House,
Great Russell Street,
London WC1B 3LS.
(For a copy of the Declaration of Intent, and their pamphlet *Pensions, the Facts.*)

British Pensioners and Trade Unions Action Association,
97 Kings Drive,
Gravesend,
Kent DA12 5BQ.

Pensioners' Voice,
91 Melling House,
Preston New Road,
Blackburn,
Lancashire BB2 6BD.

Religion

Phyllis Reeves

My leaving party had been a great success; better, I thought, than most. The presents had been marvellous, the good wishes had been given, plus the kisses and hugs from men, old and young, with whom I had hitherto had only a nodding acquaintance.

On the first morning of my retirement, I read the paper leisurely and started wondering what I was going to make of the rest of my life. I had already read several articles about retirement: I must at all costs keep fit, keep down the cholesterol, eat very little salt or fat (and no sugar, of course), and take plenty of exercise. I must also, the articles said, keep myself busily employed gardening, going to evening or day classes, having 'interests' to keep my mind active.

Fine, if I go on like this, my body will be fit for years, my mind also but have we not left out one thing: my Spirit, Soul . . . . whatever you like to call it – that something that is the real 'me'.

In our multi-racial society, most if not all Indians, West Indians and other coloured nationalities here, are reaching retirement age as firm adherents of the various faiths in which they were brought up. Unfortunately, in our so-called Christian society, this is not generally the case. We have excellent reasons for this of course. We have been too busy going to work and bringing up our families; or we were 'forced' to go to church twice each Sunday by our parents and rebelled as soon as we could. Or we just do not believe in anything anyway; partly because, with our materialistic needs supplied, we did not need to think about religion; or else we became cynical at all the misery and trouble in the world, and preferred to blame God for it, rather than ourselves or our systems. But surely at the back of our minds, is the thought that there must be more than just our short busy lives, a few years of retirement and then – nothing.

Most books and articles about retirement mention bereavement, and usually then mention some sort of religious faith, but why wait until we are bereaved and in the depths of sadness and despair, facing a bleak and lonely future because of the loss of a loved husband or wife, when so much happiness and help is there, waiting to be reached out for and taken, before bereavement and all the troubles of old age inevitably arrive. I do not think it matters at what stage in our life we seek God, or in what way, but what a waste not to experience the love of God until we seek it as a last resort to cope with the sad side of life. I am still struggling with the heartbreaking grief of losing my husband suddenly last year, but however low I feel, and it is mostly very low indeed as yet, I know for a certainty that he is in God's keeping, that he is often very near me though I cannot see him, and that one day we will meet again. I should have found that hard to believe and derive such comfort from, if I had not had a pretty sure belief in my Christian faith, gathered and experienced over many years.

But if we have neglected this aspect of our life, and I know I myself have often done this, why not start now. Start reading the psalms for their beautiful literature, the New Testament Epistles of St Paul, with his enthusiasm, to the early Church. And go to the services now and again at your local church, where you will be welcomed.

And if all this sounds too much for you, next time you go for a walk on a sunny May morning and have the good fortune to get to the top of a hill (thanks to all those keep fit exercises!) and see the beauty of our island countryside, remember and say quietly to yourself these lines of Coleridge, which I have long loved:

So will I build my altar in the fields
And the blue sky my fretted dome shall be
And the sweet fragrance that the wild flower yields
Shall be the incense I will yield to Thee,
Thee only God; and Thou shall not despise
Even me, the priest of this poor sacrifice.

Rest assured, God will hear you.

Relationships

In addition to all the other changes, retirement brings quite an upheaval in the relationship between husband and wife – as great as when the children left home, or when you first got married. Again, with a little planning, working out what each partner needs, this time can be virtually 'a prolonged second honeymoon'. Working out a plan which suits both partners' needs is never

more important than now. Some people find they yearn for a little 'space' – time and opportunity to fulfill some pursuits on their own, other retired couples are virtually inseparable. For those who have spent their working days away from the home base, the sudden change can be fairly dramatic for both sides. Until a new routine is worked out it can happen that, far from enjoying an idyllic time, little mannerisms and habits, previously unnoticed or affectionately indulged, become immensely irritating. If you have tried talking things over and seem to be getting nowhere, *do seek professional advice*. Although no two relationships are the same, the Marriage Guidance Council will have come across similar problems to yours, and looking in from the outside, they may come up with a few suggestions that had not occurred to you.

Our relationships are not, of course, confined to our husbands and wives – children, grandchildren, brothers and sisters all have an important role to play. With so many marriages ending in divorce, it is a sad fact of life that many grandparents lose touch with their grandchildren – while others 'inherit' extra grandchildren from previous marriages.

However sad or bitter you may feel about the breakdown of your child's marriage, try to remain fairly neutral. Avoid a headlong confrontation with your ex-son or ex-daughter-in-law; or you will *all* be the poorer as a result.

Relationships with grandchildren can be the most rewarding of all. Relieved of the responsibility of parenthood, grandparents are allowed a degree of indulgence, provided always that it does not cause a rift between the grandchild and its parent.

Pam Brown is a grandmother who has written a book on the subject. As she remarks: 'By the time you become a grandparent, life has knocked a lot of the stuffing out of you; worrying about money and other problems, a lot of the "magic" has gone. But grandchildren can restore that – you see things through their eyes – a bird in the garden, the beauty of a flower, things you had almost forgotten.'

She is also optimistic about the future: 'Of course you worry about children growing up in

Pam Brown.

this day and age. On the other hand, you have to be positive about the good things – at least we don't have Vikings pillaging in the back yard every other week as they used to.'

Undoubtedly the biggest upheaval, sometimes almost too awful to bear, is the loss of a husband or wife. If it has recently happened to you, you will recognize the symptoms only too well. If it has happened to someone close to you, you will recognize and understand what they are going through.

The first feeling, after the terrible shock, is likely to be complete numbness, and you may have difficulty later, recalling the exact sequence of events. This can last for several days. Others 'cope' by sub-consciously shutting it out, and then worrying frantically about trivial things – whether there will be enough sandwiches for everyone after the funeral.

Once the numbness wears off, things get worse for a while. You may feel angry – furious

even – with the person who has died and left you. You may, particularly after a long illness, feel pleased, and then feel guilty about that.

You may feel tired for no apparent reason, as well as anxious, restless and aimless. You will probably have difficulty in sleeping.

You will almost certainly get to the 'If only . . .' stage. *Everyone* who loses someone close to them thinks at some point, 'If only I'd been nicer, if only I'd listened more . . .' Remember how many times you *were* nice (and if it had been the other way around, your husband or wife would be worrying in exactly the same way about *you*).

To make matters worse, at the very time you need your family and friends most, you are likely to turn and snap at them, blaming them for all sorts of things outside their control.

After a while you may feel the need to talk about the person who has died almost incessantly (perhaps partly because we all secretly fear that if we do not pass on our little anecdotes we will forget them and they will be lost forever).

All these reactions are perfectly normal, natural and healthy.

You may not be prepared, however, for other people's reactions to you. Some people will actually cross the road to avoid you; not because they are cruel or callous, but because they do not know what to say. Others may seem stunningly insensitive when they come out with platitudes such as, 'You'll get over it', or worse, 'It's all for the best.' Do not be too hard on them, but rejoice in those rare friends who *do* encourage you to talk, to cry and to explain how you feel.

Grieving is a process that takes everyone a different length of time to get through. Elisabeth Kubler Ross, who is something of an authority on the subject, believes that you cannot speed up the process, and it is a big mistake to try. She believes that you must work through your grief, getting rid of your anger and frustration – by punching a pillow if it helps, and many have found that it does.

In cases where the husband or wife has been ill for a long time prior to death, a certain amount of grieving may already have been done – grief for the person who changed into someone you hardly knew. So do not be alarmed, conversely, if you begin to feel a lot better quite quickly – everyone seems to have their own 'time clock' when it comes to getting over a death.

But whether it takes six months or two years, you *will* begin to feel better eventually. At first it may be just for a few minutes, on one day, when you laugh and think things are not *so* bad. You may feel awful again later, but gradually the good days should begin to outnumber the bad.

Talking things over certainly does help, but if you feel you do not have anyone close enough to you, contact your local church leader, or get in touch with CRUSE, an organization to help widows, with many branches throughout Britain. Alternatively, you will find the number of The Samaritans in the telephone book.

CRUSE,
Cruse House,
126 Sheen Road,
Richmond,
Surrey.   phone: 01-940 4818

Kubler-Ross, E., *On Death and Dying; Questions and Answers on Death and Dying; To Live Until We Say Goodbye; Living with Death and Dying*
Murray Parkes, C., *Bereavement* (Pelican), £1.95.

Conclusion

Robert Dougall

For me, it is now ten years on. And as I said at the beginning, I'm still enjoying one of the most interesting times of my life. Since my autobiography, I have produced five more books, and still have my hobby of bird-watching. For the last two years I have had a marvellous time presenting Channel 4's *Years Ahead*. I feel it is a great privilege to work on this important programme and to be part of such a young, enthusiastic team.

I hope you will join us from time to time, but before I go, I would like to share a piece of advice I received from a charming lady we had on the programme in the early days.

'As long as you're rolling the dice,' she said, 'you're still in the game . . .'

How right she is.

Address List

Age Concern

Age Concern is a registered charity (formerly The National Old People's Welfare Council) whose broad objective is to promote the welfare of elderly people. It has over 1,300 local groups throughout Britain who work with volunteers to provide a number of services. They also have a long list of publications covering almost every aspect of life in retirement. For more details of your nearest branch look in the telephone book under 'Age Concern' or 'Old People's Welfare', or contact:

Age Concern England,
Bernard Sunley House,
60 Pitcairn Road,
Mitcham,
Surrey CR4 3LL.   phone: 01-640-5431

Age Concern Northern Ireland,
128 Victoria Street,
Belfast BT2 7BG.   phone: 0232-245729

Age Concern Scotland,
33 Castle Street,
Edinburgh EH2 3DN.   phone: 031-225-5000

Age Concern Wales,
1 Park Grove,
Cardiff CF1 3BJ.   phone: 0222-371566

Disability Alliance,
21 Star Street,
London W2 1QB.   phone: 01-402-7026

Choice Magazine – the only magazine for retirement planning. 70p each month from newsagents, or on subscription.

Choice Magazine,
Bedford Chambers,
Covent Garden,
London WC2E 8HA.

Citizens' Advice Bureau (CAB)

There are over 800 branches throughout the country, who are able to help and advise on a huge range of problems and difficulties. To find out where your nearest branch is look under 'C' in the telephone book or ask at the library or town hall.

Contact

There are many contact groups all over Britain. They aim to provide companionship, and usually meet about once a month.
Contact,
15 Henrietta Street,
Covent Garden,
London WC2 8QA.   phone: 01-240-0630

Centre for Policy on Ageing,
Nuffield Lodge,
Regents Park,
London NW1 4RS.   phone: 01-722-8871

Yours magazine, published monthly by Help The Aged. It contains information on health, sport, leisure activities, and political issues that affect pensioners.
Yours,
PO Box 126,
Watford WD1 2HG.

Help The Aged,
32 Dover Street,
London W1.

Disabled Living Foundation,
Information Services,
346 Kensington High Street,
London W14 8NS

Royal Association for Disability and Rehabilitation (RADAR),
25 Mortimer Street,
London W1N 8AB

Index

STOP PRESS

PENSIONS

P.38 The annual rises in state pensions and other benefits will not be announced until June 1984. They will be based on the May inflation figure which it is *estimated* will be in the region of 5 to 5.5 per cent. The increases come into effect in November 1984.

	Until November 1984:	Estimated new figures between:
Basic pension		
single person	£34.05	£35.75-35.92
married couple	£54.50	£57.23-57.50
wife on husband's contributions	£20.45	£21.47-21.57
Supplementary pension		
single person	£34.10	£35.81-35.98
married couple	£54.55	£57.28-57.55
Earnings rule	£65.00	no change
Widow's allowance (for first 26 weeks)	£47.65	£50.03-50.27
plus for each child	£7.60	£7.98-8.02
Mobility allowance	£19.00	£19.95-20.05
Invalidity benefit	£32.60	£34.23-34.39
adult dependent	£19.55	£20.53-20.63
Attendance allowance		
night and day	£27.20	£28.56-28.70
night only or day only	£18.15	£19.06-19.15
Invalid care allowance		
self	£20.45	£21.47-21.57
wife/housekeeper	£12.25	£12.86-12.92
each child	£7.60	£7.98-8.02

DHSS leaflet NI 196 gives details of the rates payable on all social security benefits, and leaflet FB2 gives information about all the different types of benefit and allowances. Both are available free from your DHSS office.

P.43 TAX

	1983/4	1984/5
Personal allowance (under 65)		
single person	£1,785	£2,005
married couple	£2,795	£3,155
Age allowance (over 65)		
single person	£2,360	£2,490
married couple	£3,755	£3,955
Age allowance income limit	£7,600	£8,100
Additional personal allowance	£1,010	£1,150
Widow's bereavement allowance	£1,010	£1,150

Housekeeper allowance	£100	
Son's or daughter's help	£55	
Dependent relative		no change
single woman	£145	
other	£100	
Blind person's	£360	

SAVINGS

Investment Income Surcharge has now been abolished.

Monthly Income Bonds	previous limit:	from March 15th 1984:
	£200,000	£50,000
Investment accounts	previous limit:	from May 1984:
	£200,000	£50,000

Bank interest New plans for interest on bank accounts to be paid with tax already deducted were announced in the March 1984 budget. From April 1985 they will operate on a similar basis to building society savings accounts. Your local branch will be able to give you further information.

Stamp Duty Cut from 2% to 1% in March 1984. Also, Stamp Duty is only payable on property transfers above £30,000.

Capital Gains Tax	1983/4	1984/5
Exemption limit	£5,300	£5,600
Capital Transfer Tax	1983/4	1984/5
Lifetime transfer started at	£60,001	£64,001
	15%-50%	15%-30%
Death transfer started at	£60,001	£64,001
	30%-60%	no change

Main exemptions from Capital Transfer Tax	
small gifts to anyone	£250
annual exemption	£3,000
wedding gifts by parents	£5,000
grandparents	£2,000
anyone else	£1,000

Life assurance premiums Tax relief is no longer given on premiums for life assurance policies taken out after 13th March, 1984. Policies taken out before that date are *not* affected.

Change of address:
National Association of Carers,
Lilac House,
Medway Homes,
Balfour Road,
Rochester,
Kent ME4 6QU.   phone: Medway (0634) 813981